COCKLOFT

COCKLOFT

Scenes
From
A
Gay Marriage

Kyle Thomas Smith

Columbus, Ohio

Cockloft: Scenes From a Gay Marriage

Published by Gatekeeper Press
2167 Stringtown Rd, Suite 109
Columbus, OH 43123-2989
www.GatekeeperPress.com

Copyright © 2018 by Kyle Thomas Smith
All rights reserved. Neither this book, nor any parts within it may be sold or reproduced in any form or by any electronic or mechanical means, including information storage and retrieval systems without permission in writing from the author. The only exception is by a reviewer, who may quote short excerpts in a review.

ISBN: 9781642372168
eISBN: 9781642372175

Printed in the United States of America

In memory of our dear departed Marquez (April 2004 – July 20, 2017), the little Tuxedo cat whose beauty and loveliness were as boundless and timeless as our love for him.

Our relationships with one another are like a chance meeting of two strangers in a parking lot. They look at each other and smile. That is all there is between them. They leave and never see each other again. That is what life is—just a moment, a passing and then it is gone.

—H.E. Chagdud Tulku Rinpoche

When I married Miles, we were both a couple of maladjusted misfits. We are still maladjusted misfits, and we have loved every minute of it.

—Stella, *Rear Window*

CONTENTS

Cockloft 15
Don Paco Pepe 23
A Brooklyn Haiku 26
Finger-Twirling: The World's Oldest Profession? 27
Memory Sparked During the Week Prince Died 34
An Impossibility 37
The Cherry Blossoms 39
Trinity 40
The Biggest Weirdo 52
A Name I Will Never Forget 54
Compliance 55
That's Amore! Delle Palle! 56
The Universe 62
Islanders & Alligators 64
An Attractive Nuisance 68
Profundity 71
Delusions of Grandeur 73
Zero Dark Squirrelly: Cockloft, Part II 75
Center-Stage 82
Casual Coercion 83
7 Mississippi 84
Le Journal d'Une Femme de Chambre—Montréal 85
Cutpurse 87
Wide-Eyed 88
The Mandarins 89

Paris Birthday	90
"Is This One of those Buddhist Meditations?"	91
Wide-Eyed, The Prequel	96
Fountain of the Peeing Boy in Footie Pajamas: An Introduction to Logic	97
Rattrapage	104
A Reminder to Always Take a Deep Breath Before Taking Offense	105
Etymology	106
How Are You Going to Handle the End of the World?	107
The Secret Lives of Santorumites	109
Raindrops Drip off Iron Bars	111
The King & I	113
Scruffy AristoCat	114
Thick & Thin	122
Steeplechase	123
Vocabulary Builders	124
MT	126
The Filipino Nurse	127
Socialism	130
Self-Parenting (Like a Total Dork)	131
Pontius Pilates	134
The Profanation of St. Francis	136
Sei Italiano?	138
An Audience of Teletubbies	140
Swingers	141
The Alpaca Guy	142
The Zafu Apocalypse	144
Mudder	145
Julius Prepares the Joint Tax Return	146
Nature	149
Breakfasts & Nightmares	150
Distinction	151

Another Brexit Nightmare	152
Bang Yer Head	156
One Month After Brexit	157
Collusion	158
Oudeschans: An Ex-Altar Boy Hashes It Out with God On the Edge of the Red Light District	159
N the House	190
Pangloss: Worry Jar, Part I	191
French Phone By the Bed	192
The Medium at the Fireman's Ball	194
Gymnopedie	197
Ashes to Paste: Worry Jar, Part II	199
Copenhagen	201
Home from Denmark & A Funeral in Chicago	203
Calcutta, Ohio	204
Apropos	206
Almodovar or the Animal Hospital?	207
Kali Yuga	208
Tormentor	213
Aristophanes, Remembered	214
Touché	215
A Party	217
Later at the Party	218
The Man Upstairs	219
Caesar for Two	223
The Comey Letter	225
Bar Boulud	226
Template Noir	227
Old Canarsie	229
A Rippling Cascade	231
Treadmill Tonglen	232
Train Gauge	234
Dr. Goldberg's Office	235

Non-Self 237
Cats at the Dawn of the Trump-Russia
Administration 238
Connoisseur, Come Back to Earth 241
Kyle Pines for a More Diverse Gene Pool 242
As Hope Prepares to Leave Office 245
Thanksgiving Anyway 246
Wiggle Room 247
Julius Offers Additional Training to
the Substitute Cleaning Lady 249
Duck Soup 251
Water Buffalos 252
A Sackful of Gold 253
Monkeys Mate Outside the Dumbulla
Cave Temple in Sri Lanka 254
Counteractive 255
A Man Lives on a High-School Teacher's
Salary in Europe 257
New Years Eve, Sri Lanka 258
The Frankfurt School 260
The Zaftig Hildegard 261
Twilight Walk through Montreal's Old City 263
Ice Block 264
Epiphany 266
Tastes Change 268
In a Kornfield with Rudy Giuliani 270
Protégé 273
Technical Assistance with the Dead 274
Dor 276
The Leopard at Des Artistes 279
The Post-Structuralist Mafia 280
Slack 282
The Lower Haight 284
The Snake Pit 285

The London Psychic 288
Exeunt 289
The Theatre Lofts: A Three-Ring Epilogue 291
Afterword: Mini-Pizza Bagels And The
Real Masterpiece 296
Author Bio 315
Acknowledgments 317

COCKLOFT

Some guys just shouldn't have a cockloft.
    And it turns out, Julius and I are two of them.
    Until yesterday, I didn't even know what a cockloft is.
    I'd been meditating on our top floor and both the cats were with me. I kept hearing all this scratching on the closet door behind me but I thought it was Giuseppe, our Tabby, playing around. He'd never shown any interest in the closet door before, but I thought this must be one of his new things and I didn't want to break my concentration, so I continued focusing on my breath and gathering back my awareness of the present moment.
    Boy, there was a lot of scratching going on, though.
    And since I meditate with my eyes open, Zen-style, I couldn't help but notice that my other cat Marquez was staring at me with his ears pricked up but I thought Marquez was just acting dramatic over Giuseppe being crazy with the door. Soon, though, Giuseppe walked up from behind me, looking every bit as alarmed as Marquez, and the scratching hadn't stopped.

As soon as my meditation timer rang, I got off the cushion and kept hearing all this scurrying. I didn't think it was a burglar since our alarm system would've let me know, but I kept hearing it.

I walked into the hallway and looked up at the ceiling above our staircase. Right above me a squirrel was tap-dancing on the plate-glass sunroof. As I stood transfixed, Julius called from Washington, where he'd been working all week.

I told him I was by the staircase looking up at the squirrel's belly.

He said, "Oh, that's bad. If it's above the staircase, that means it's in the cockloft."

"What's a cockloft?"

He said it's that aluminum-and-glass contraption we have on the roof, which is full of insulation and electrical wires. It's supposed to be sealed shut but somehow the squirrel got in. They call it a cockloft because it resembles a rooster's lookout for available hens on his horny days.

Already it was sounding like something we had no business being the owners of.

We called Animal Care and Control and they put us in touch with Allstate Animal Control, who said they could send some guys out to do a catch-and-release on Sunday.

Now Julius was on the verge of heart failure.

The squirrel could get at the wires.

Or it could die in the cockloft with no food and water.

Or it might be nesting and having babies even as we speak.

After a lot of back and forth, Julius managed to rattle enough cages to get Allstate to send somebody over that same afternoon. He booked an emergency ticket and flew in on the two o'clock shuttle.

By 4:00 p.m., we were both home.

We went upstairs and looked above the stairs to the cockloft's plate-glass floor.

We didn't see a squirrel, but that didn't necessarily mean it wasn't there. It might have been in a corner we couldn't see. We hoped the Allstate guys could find it, catch it and set it free in Prospect Park.

We went back to the room where I'd been meditating.

I opened the door to the closet that Giuseppe had been expressing undue interest in. Julius clicked on his iPhone's flashlight app which revealed claw and paw prints all over the closet walls. We also saw that the squirrel had kicked in a board that had blocked an insulated passageway. The squirrel must have broken into the closet but then gotten scared and rambled back into the cockloft.

All we could do now was wait for the animal-control guys.

We walked downstairs to our kitchen. Julius started fixing himself a sandwich and I started doing some dishes. We talked about whether we should keep taking the cats to the same vet or whether we should start taking them to one of those Park Avenue vets who charge a lot more but also set cats up with longevity plans and do extra tests to ensure that absolutely everything's up to snuff with them.

As we were talking, Giuseppe came trotting in. He was running something into a corner and it wasn't his new Nobbly Wobbly toy.

"Shit! JULIUS! He's with the squirrel!"

Julius flinched: "WHAT? Wait, what's the matter?"

I bolted out our kitchen's saloon door with a sponge and soapy glass in my hand, "GIUSEPPE'S WITH THE SQUIRRRRRREL!!!"

Julius whipped around, "What? Where?"

Julius spotted the beast on the other side of the fern, where Giuseppe had it cornered.

Julius let out a scream that all but stopped traffic on Third Street.

Wailing in unison, we booked it into the dining room, slamming the door behind us. While we were so busy flailing our arms and running around our dining-room table like Girl Scouts on meth, we'd lost sight of the fact that we'd left Giuseppe in the kitchen with the intruder. Catching our breaths, we tiptoed back and opened the door about as much as our primordial fears of vermin would allow.

The cat came flying out. Realizing he'd come face to face with an interloper from the animal kingdom, Giuseppe, who'd once slugged it out in brawls at the ASPCA, proceeded to go catatonic with shock on the Oriental rug.

Only one thing was certain: This situation wasn't going to improve until we manned up—or at least did something worthy of being cockloft owners.

I locked Marquez and Giuseppe in the upstairs library, came back downstairs and posted open the door that leads from the kitchen to the gangway, hoping the damn varmint would scurry out of our lives for good.

Julius normally assumes command in the various crises we've had to face together, but standing in the kitchen with a squirrel bounding from one end of the room to the other, he utterly fell apart. Hopping up and down in his slick Gregory Peck pinstriped suit, he kept screeching, "Wadda I do? Wadda I do?"

I said, "Jesus, Julius, how 'bout opening the window? I'll go man the door." (And, for this situation, I used the term "man" loosely.)

All skin and bones and spiny tail, the rodent alternately scampered and scavenged on top of and on all sides of our kitchen table. Julius had long thrown open the window but this thing wasn't moving anywhere in the direction of outside.

Wincing as I held the gangway door open with my back, the only sound that seemed to fill my ears were those of Julius's admonitions to the trespasser:

"Don't you eat my geraniums!"

"*Hey! Those are my persimmons, not yours! Stop eating them!*"

For lack of a lion tamer's chair, I handed Julius a slab of cardboard from a PetCo box, which he used as a shield as he jumped at the squirrel and back.

And at it and back.
And at it and back.
But mostly back.

I watched in fascinated horror as the squirrel ignored him.

After investigating all of our baskets and pots, the beast flashed like a furry, sanguinary, sharp-clawed laser from one end of the room to the other with all the pandemonium of a bat in the glare of a spelunker's torch.

Until at last it'd made up its mind that it'd had enough and sauntered out the window with the ease of Bette Davis crossing a penthouse living room to fix herself a nightcap.

As it took a nice cool drink of water by our gangway's koi pond, Julius shut both the window screen and window with a crash. A real cockloft owner would have added, "And stay out!"

But not us.

We were well-aware that, out of all the beings under our roof that day, Giuseppe was the one who had shown the most valor.

The Allstate animal-control guys showed up at the front door about half an hour later. They were two big Blutos from Staten Island, wearing hoodies and construction boots.

Planting himself smack in the center of our living room's parquet floors, the foreman, a Dan Conner doppelganger, hooked his thumbs into the side-straps of his slate-gray *Metropolis* jumpsuit, heralding, "We understand ya got a problem here."

His assistant, who was about as big as the foreman, wore a five o'clock shadow and a Skinny Pete hat. Tossing a Medieval-looking metal trap from one hand to the other, Skinny Pete said, "Lead the way, boss." They strode over to the stairs with the sangfroid of guys who wrestle raccoons barehanded for sport, each with one hand tied behind their back.

Sizing up every corner of our walls, Dan Conner plunked down a ladder once we brought him to the sunroof. He climbed into the cockloft and whipped out a flashlight to inspect its every nook and cranny.

"Nutin's up there," he said, "No squirrels. No rats."

Eyes flaring at the word "rats," Skinny Pete ran the tip of his tongue across his top row of teeth. He climbed up next, clanging the trap against his thigh like a tambourine. After giving the cockloft another set of eyes, he sighed, "Ya fine. Lemme just double-seal some spots. Hope the squirrel ain't opened up his mouth 'bout what a lovely home ya got here."

"Nah," said Dan Conner, first to Skinny Pete and then to us, "Ain't nutin' up there."

It was a relief for Julius and me to know that we weren't going to be finding anything the next time we'd go feeling around our cockloft.

DON PACO PEPE

(Julius enters kitchen. Finds Kyle in a weeping heap.)

JULIUS: Kyle! What . . . Oh, no. It was workshop night.

KYLE: They said my play was so sedentary, it makes *My Dinner with Andre* look like *The Matrix*.

JULIUS: Now, Kyle, did they really say that?

KYLE: They might as well have. They said it takes more than wisecracks and banter to make a play go round. They say it needs a plot. A plot! I mean, what do these people want from me?

JULIUS: You mean, besides a plot?

KYLE: Well isn't that the trouble with this world? People are all busy, busy, busy—rushing, rushing, rushing to whatever distraction they can find next.—What about stillness, huh? What about rumination? What about plumbing one's depths? What about appreciating the multidimensionality of the moment? My meditation group would be all over it.

JULIUS: Kyle, when I was growing up in Puerto Rico, my aunt used to tell me the parable of Don Paco Pepe.

KYLE: Oh no! Not the Donkey Story again!

JULIUS: Yes, the Donkey Story again.—Don Paco Pepe was going into town with his grandson. It was a long walk so Don Paco Pepe picked up his grandson and put his grandson on to his donkey and as Don Paco Pepe walked alongside the donkey, Don Paco Pepe and his grandson made their way on the long, dusty roads into town. *Well!* People along the way were beside themselves! "Don Paco Pepe," they said, "You're an old man. You should take a load off. You ride the donkey. Your grandson is old enough to walk to town on his own two feet." So Don Paco Pepe took his grandson off the donkey and then Don Paco Pepe climbed on to the donkey and then Don Paco Pepe and his grandson and the donkey started back on their way to town. Up the road, they saw another group of people and these people were just as scandalized as the first group of people, except these people said, "Don Paco Pepe, how can you be so cruel to that poor donkey? It is far too small and you are far too big." Well, Don Paco Pepe knew he couldn't keep riding the donkey or people would be mad at him. And Don Paco Pepe knew he couldn't let his grandson ride the donkey or people would be mad at both Don Paco Pepe *and* his grandson. So Don Paco Pepe did the only thing left to do. Don Paco Pepe got off the donkey and Don Paco Pepe picked up the donkey and Don Paco Pepe carried the donkey into town. And the moral of the story is . . . ?

JULIUS & KYLE: *(in unison—Julius, exultant; Kyle, blasé)* That if you're out to please everyone, you're in for a hernia.

JULIUS: That's right.

(Beat)

KYLE: Julius . . . I never told you this but . . . that is bar-none the DUMBEST story I've ever heard in my entire life.

JULIUS: Oh, really, Kyle? Well at least it has a plot.

(Julius storms out of the kitchen.)

A Brooklyn Haiku

A call-girl rang our doorbell at 3:30 this morning.

Julius answered the door in salmon-colored pajamas.

That's when she knew she had the wrong house.

FINGER-TWIRLING:
THE WORLD'S OLDEST PROFESSION?

This is for discrimination and egotists who think supreme
And this is for whoever taught you
how to kiss in designer jeans.
—Prince, "Lady Cab Driver"

For a long time, Mom blamed herself for my bad grades in school. She was already exhausted enough, raising a houseful of six kids when I happened along, quite by surprise. So, when I was supposed to be learning Reading, 'Riting, 'Rithmetic with The Count, Big Bird, and a chaser of *The Electric Company*, she didn't protest too much when my siblings would come along and change the channel to *General Hospital, What's Happening!!, Soap*, or those reprehensible *ABC After-School Specials*.

But, the way I see it, this was no tragedy. In time, I became a devoted reader and writer. (I still suck at math.) Plus, overexposure to junk culture gave me a whole different jumping-off point from kids who were weaned on *Sesame Street*.

For instance, I developed an early fascination with Urban Fiction from Blaxploitation films, which were constantly airing (replete with bleeps and scene edits) in the late Seventies, especially on the U-Channels and Insomniac Theater. I sat through more of them than I can count—*Blacula, Cleopatra Jones, Superfly, Shaft, Foxy Brown*. (Note: those were different times; I was too young to have a social conscience about what I was watching, and Mom was in the other room.) These movies were rife with guns, pushers, pimps and crooked cops.

But the hookers were the ones who fascinated me most.

I didn't know what they were doing. I knew they enticed men, but I didn't know for what purpose.

To me, they were just strange women, standing on street corners in tight minis, often while leaning against brick buildings under elevated subway tracks, twirling the dangling ends of their chain-link belts.

I knew they twirled chains. I had no idea what they were up to past that.

One Saturday morning, I was with Mom and my sister Kathy in the kitchen. As usual, the TV was blaring. Channel 7 *Eye-Witness News* was on. Kathy was wearing her canary yellow terrycloth robe and burning a Cheddar omelet on the General Electric stove. Mom was wearing a black apron with white polka dots and pouring Cascade into our new dishwasher. I was sitting at the table, drinking an iceless Lipton Iced Tea that I'd mixed myself from a bottle, which had a warning label on it, which read that the beverage I was enjoying was laced with something called saccharine, which was responsible for the deaths of laboratory animals.

The anchorman announced that the National Hookers Convention in Las Vegas was in full-swing.

Mom noted her disdain with a scowl.

My sister responded with a smirk and the gambit, "It's the world's oldest profession, *Mom*."

"Next to motherhood," Mom countered.

The camera flashed to a dais of women who looked just like the ones from those movies.

My eyes dilated, "What's a profession?"

Kathy snarled out the side of her mouth, "It's how you make your money."

Catching sight of my awe, Mom said, "Kathleen, turn that smut off *now*!"

Kathy complied, knowing she'd won the match. Her youngest brother had learned what the world's oldest profession is.

I remember going away from the table that day, meditating on olden times. You see, in addition to *Superfly*, I was also fond of 1950's Bible epics like *Ben Hur*, *The Egyptian* and *The Ten Commandments*. Those films were strewn with pharaohs, shepherds, Romans and Hebrews. (I guess there were harlots in them too, but these were G-rated movies, so a five-year-old couldn't tell.) I began to put two and two together. So, there were hookers in the times of the pharaohs and the shepherds, huh?

A picture began to form in my mind.

For years after that, I walked around imagining bearded men in caftans, carrying staffs through the scorching desert...and passing by women, who were in pumps and purple, Saran-Wrap mini-skirts, twirling chains from their hips.

One thing I did have in common with other kids was that I loved Superheroes. I watched every cartoon and live-action show on the air. I wore the pages out on my Marvel Comic Books. I wore out whatever Underoos Mom would buy me for my birthday. The Hall of Justice and the Legion of Doom had timeshares on my heart. Linda Carter was a goddess as Wonder Woman: her invisible jet (but you could still see *her* in it, so what was the point?), her golden lasso, her bulletproof bracelets, and don't forget that twirl for those costume changes (I used to wonder, if you pulled her out of the pyrotechnics, mid-twirl, would she be naked?). The Wonder Twins were a vision of metamorphosis and possibilities in life. I would have traded all my siblings in lock, stock and barrel to have had Christopher Reeves as my older brother.

Now, mind you, I did not feel that way about every superhero. While I would certainly watch *Batman*, Adam West had love handles, so I considered him inadequate, and Robin was just a twerp no matter which way you sliced him.

But Captain Marvel!

Now *that* was a Man.

Some rippling guy named John Davey played him on the series *Shazam!*, which ran for three seasons before going into reruns. The show was about a teenage boy and his Mentor, who traveled in a Winnebago to wherever there was trouble. Whenever they saw things getting out of hand, the teenager just had to shout, "Shazam!" and The World's Mightiest Mortal, Captain Marvel, would dive from the sky to save the day (if you looked closely enough, you could see strings attached). Then all the characters would stand around dumbfounded at how well everything worked out. As if that weren't enough, at show's end, Captain Marvel would make an encore appearance to deliver a Public Service Announcement, which always gave you one to grow on.

I never missed a *Shazam!* rerun. John Davey was too good to pass up. (By the way, I just Googled him and couldn't find anything he did after *Shazam!*.) He had a torso like an iceberg, which that nylon suit did nothing to hide. Man, they knew what they were doing in Wardrobe. All across America, teenyboppers were dropping issues of *Tiger Beat* to tune in. I was probably the only boy on the block, though, who was planning my wedding to John Davey.

Not that I could tell my brothers this.

One Saturday morning, I wanted to be alone with Captain Marvel. Our basement's red and black argyle-patterned carpet was burning my bare legs as I geared up for the weekly *Shazam!* episode under our red plastic-plated ceiling lamps. I dressed up for the occasion in tan short shorts and a black t-shirt that featured a Crocodile holding a tennis racket.

The theme song started up.

And, wouldn't you know, my brothers Kerry and Kevin just had to come down to join me. I paid them no mind and trained my attention on John Davey instead. It must have been a splendid episode. I remember jumping to my feet and giving it a rousing ovation.

A Tide commercial came on.

Kevin was curling the twenty-pound dumbbells that Dad had bought at Sportmart that week and Kerry was counting his chin-ups on the chin-up bar that he'd fastened in the doorway to our workroom.

Shazam! came back on.

It was time for Captain Marvel to give his PSA.

I stood at attention.

Captain Marvel swooped down from the sky, landing squarely on his feet.

"Hi," he said.

In an instant, I summoned all that I had learned from the women in *Shaft*, *Foxy Brown*, and countless other bad-influence movies. I shifted my weight to my left leg, put my hand on my left hip, cocked my head to the right and, simulating the way those women in those movies twirled their chains, started twirling my right index finger. Then, instead of saying hi back to Captain Marvel, I did him one better and I said "Hoy-oy-oy-oy."

The room fell silent.

Kevin put down the dumbbell. Kerry let go of the chin-up bar. They looked at each other. They looked at me. Within three seconds, our house shook with laughter.

Twirling one's index finger and saying, "Hoy-oy-oy-oy," became standard greeting among the kids in our house.

I never told them that I had adapted the gesture from the night moves of ladies of the evening and that, when I first used it, I was trying to seduce Captain Marvel.

By the mid-Eighties, my sister Colleen had an executive position in the public-relations department of a bank on LaSalle Street. Like other members of my family, she had grown so accustomed to twirling her finger and saying "Hoy-oy-oy-oy" that she had even begun using the salutation among her colleagues in corporate America. Soon they were twirling their fingers and saying "Hoy-oy-oy-oy" to each other too.

In 1989, I pulled some strings and, though I was underage, landed a part-time job as a messenger for Record Copy Services, which was also on LaSalle Street next door to where Colleen worked. One afternoon, I walked into her office building's lobby with a package for a law firm. As I stood at the elevator bank, I observed a woman in a navy-blue business suit stepping off an elevator. She seemed to recognize another woman walking toward her in a similar business suit.

"Jane," the woman called out.

"Mary," the other woman responded.

Then they both twirled their fingers and said, "Hoy-oy-oy-oy."

I looked down at the lobby's marble floor and quickly boarded the elevator. I didn't have the nerve to tell the two businesswomen that they were acting like hookers.

MEMORY SPARKED DURING THE WEEK PRINCE DIED

(*It's 1985. After putting 4-1-1 charges on to his parents' phone bill, Kyle, age 11, makes a long-distance call to the offices of* Seventeen *magazine in New York City.*)

RECEPTIONIST: *Seventeen* magazine. How may I direct your call?

KYLE: Hello. My name is Kyle Smith. I'm calling from Chicago, Illinois and have I got an idea for you!

RECEPTIONIST: You have an idea for me?

KYLE: Yes. I've been watching your commercials and... well, you know that song on the radio by Chaka Khan, "I Feel For You."

RECEPTIONIST: Yes. It was originally a Prince song.

KYLE: Was it? Wow! I love Prince.—Well, I mean, I don't LOVE Prince because that would be gay...but we play him while my sister is getting ready for dates and we do her makeup.

RECEPTIONIST: *We* do her makeup?

KYLE: Yeah. I help.

RECEPTIONIST: *(deadpan)* Oh, the girls are gonna love you when you grow up.

KYLE: Thanks. They're already starting to. But to get back to my point, I know how you can sell more magazines.

RECEPTIONIST: How?

KYLE: With this song I made up.

RECEPTIONIST: I'm listening.

KYLE: So, you know how that guy starts the song by going, "Chaka Khan/Chaka Khan/Chaka Khan."— By the way, did you know that Chaka Khan is from Chicago? And I'm from Chicago—

RECEPTIONIST: I know. You said that. Get on with your song.

KYLE: Well, instead of saying, "Chaka Khan," the guy will say, *(Kyle breaks into a rap)* "*Seventeen/Seventeen/Seventeen/Seventeen* magazine/That's what you wanna read/It's what you wanna read/When you wanna be a teen."

RECEPTIONIST: That's it?

KYLE: Well, I haven't worked it all out. But, yeah.— And then Chaka comes on and she sings *(Kyle croons)*, "Baby, baby, when I flip through you . . ."

RECEPTIONIST: Let me stop you right there. We don't take these ideas over the phone.

KYLE: Oh, I'm just getting warmed up.

RECEPTIONIST: Listen, write it down or better yet *record* it, mail it to us and I'll send it to our marketing department for consideration.

KYLE: Deal!

> (**Author's Note:** I was too lazy to go ahead and write or record the jingle but that didn't stop me from telling all the kids at school that I was going to be teaming up with Chaka Khan on the new *Seventeen* magazine commercial and that Prince was going to be singing backup. "We had to let him," I told them, "I mean, it *was* his song.")

AN IMPOSSIBILITY

(*September 2015*)

JULIUS: Kyle, this has got to stop. You woke up in a sweating panic. You'll see. Donald Trump will not be president.

KYLE: You don't know that. My dreams are often prophetic. And not only that, I . . . I had a sex dream, Julius.

JULIUS: Oh no! With Trump?

KYLE: Worse. Bill O'Reilly.

JULIUS: Oh Jesus!

KYLE: Hey, that's what he said!—It was dark. He walked into our room. I was naked on the bed. And I said, "Oh, Bill…You're not the only one who knows how to double down on horrendous positions."

JULIUS: (*dancing out the heebie jeebies*) Eeew!

KYLE: Does it leave you concerned about the future of our country?

JULIUS: No. That line leaves me concerned about your future as a writer.

KYLE: But I can't be held responsible for what I say or do in dreams. Just in real life. I, Kyle Thomas Smith, making love to Bill O'Reilly? What do you think that means in real life?

JULIUS: Well, it means we're not having dinner anywhere near Rockefeller Center tonight.

THE CHERRY BLOSSOMS

Julius called me from Tokyo this morning. He said his coworkers dragged him to a bar in the Roppongi district last night to watch Japan's roughest, toughest rugby team, The Cherry Blossoms, go head to head with Scotland. The Cherry Blossoms lost. Julius was half-expecting this. What he was not expecting was that these guys he works with, who are as ceremonious as a royal retinue at the office, go buck-fucking ballistic when they watch rugby. Meanwhile, Julius was sitting on a bar stool with his hands folded like he's about to break out opera glasses but these guys kept scooping him into bear hugs and body-surfing him around the room. By the time The Cherry Blossoms scored their last goal, Julius saw Koki from accounting coming for him. Julius put his hands up like stop signs and said, "Look, Koki, we need to set a boundary." Koki found someone else to grab. Julius ducked out of the bar and started walking back to his hotel. He passed a club where the bouncer said, "Kama sutra service." Julius kept walking. A guy passing out flyers for another club said, "Titties in your face." Julius said, "I'd rather see the cherry blossoms." So this morning, he went to the botanical gardens.

TRINITY

It's autumn in New York and, all weekend, stoop sales abound in my Brooklyn neighborhood. On every third or fourth stoop there sits a fat, crumbling paperback of *Atlas Shrugged*, never on sale for more than a quarter and almost always counterbalanced by something more socially conscious like Ta-Nehisi Coates or something more urbane like Gore Vidal. This is the brownstone dweller's way of telegraphing to the liberal-progressive neighborhood that Ayn Rand was merely a morbid curiosity whose work, once indulged, could be sold away at an insulting price. I've witnessed this trend every September for the past 15 years, so I no longer balk.

Today, though, I just had to stop when I saw that one stoop on President Street was serving up a whole other kind of paperback. Seeing it took me back to childhood in much the same way that the Madeleine took Proust back to Combray.

The book was Leon Uris's *Trinity*.

For most Irish, *Trinity* evokes visions of strife between Catholics and Protestants, natives and Brits, the shanty and the lace curtain in the motherland. For me, it evokes memories of my sister Kathy letting me wear her hot-pink lipstick and electric-blue eye shadow as she'd tell me about her boyfriends at her makeup table in the early eighties.

"No, you're doing it all wrong," she'd say, dousing a cotton swab with Walgreen's rubbing alcohol. Wiping away the blue smear from underneath my eye, she said on one particular day, "Should put ya out in the Forest Preserve and let ya clan up with the raccoons, is what I should do. Would ya stop fidgeting already! Jesus! So, anyway, his name is Nigel. Nigel Smith, can ya believe it?"

The *Flashdance* soundtrack was playing in the background. Kathy was 21 and had moved back home for a while. By day, she worked at the Apparel Center downtown and would come back from work, raring to scandalize Mom with scuttlebutt from all the gay designers she worked with, "They're all dating priests, Mom! Every swooshin' one of 'em!"

"Oh, dear," Mom would anguish, a spatula rattling in her hand.

"I said to 'em, 'Priests?' Nah, c'mon. Ya mean the guys who say Mass?' And then they said…" at this Kathy would pause to let her wrist go limp as she'd jut out her hip and strike the pose of a hooker asking a sailor for a light, "'Come now, K*aaa*athy, don't be so naiiiiiive.'"

Whenever Kathy said things like this, Mom would close her eyes, clutch the counter and shake her head as if to cast Kathy's insinuation forever out of her mind. Kathy would stand with her arms folded, lovin' every minute of it.

As for me, I would step back and take it all in. If Kathy's stories were anything to go by, there was a friskier world going on out there than the one I'd known at the Y or at St. Mary of the Woods or in Mom's kitchen. Kathy hadn't taken to fixing my makeup so much because she'd noticed I was becoming like those priest-daters at the Apparel Center, although given the relish with which I'd apply it, I'm sure the thought was never far from her mind; rather, she wanted to make sure I'd make a real entrance the next time I'd go on a beer run for her to the basement fridge. The refrigerator was on the other side of Dad's La-Z-Boy chair. Her hope was that he'd wake up snorting like a molested walrus when he'd see me riffling through the bottom shelf and darting back up the stairs like a beer-toting wood sprite in drag. Dad hadn't woken up on the night Kathy first mentioned Nigel Smith, though. No matter, the Miller Lite was now cold in Kathy's coaster and she had christened the rim with a fresh coat of lipstick.

"Nigel Smith," she said, "Same last name as us. But he's English."

I jolted, "You mean, like those people on Channel 11?"

"Yep," she said, "I met him at Haggerty's. I was there with Doreen. You get a free pitcher if you win the dance-off, so one of us tries to win it every time it's our turn to buy a round. They were playing this song right here, actually, when I won."

The *Flashdance* soundtrack was now on "He's A Dream." I'd watched *Flashdance* with Kathy on her Betamax once. All it took was that one viewing for me to recall that it was at this point in the movie that, after doing a rollicking striptease, Jennifer Beals stations herself on the edge of a chair, reels back, and fans out her legs. The sequence all but freezes as her body double tugs the rope on a bucket that's teetering on a scaffold and blast after blast of water comes crashing down on to her scantily clad frame, all to the delight of the Pittsburgh spot-welders sitting ringside at the cabaret tables.

Now, I'm not saying Kathy did any of these things at Haggerty's dance-off. These were purely hallucinations of my callow mind—hallucinations informed by content that had clearly slipped past the censors. Nor was I planning on using these fantasies as any sort of blackmail against Kathy, who wouldn't have been allowed to live in our house if there were even the faintest rumor that she was running around town in a wet t-shirt. I was just jealous that Kathy might have had the chance to reenact Jennifer Beal's bedraggled burlesque show on a boozy catwalk.

Oh, to be a fly on the wall of those singles bars she'd describe! And to get to wear what she got to wear to them—like that chunky necklace full of Lego trinkets. I'd once overheard Kathy telling my cousin Jeannie that she'd been wearing the Lego necklace on the elevator at the Apparel Center when Madonna happened to step on and ask her, "Hey! Where'd ya buy that, honey?"

Sometime later I said to Kathy, "Tell it again. Tell me how you met Madonna."

She said, "Met Madonna? What the hell are you talking about?"

So the gift of Blarney was most likely the driving force behind most of her stories. But I didn't care, just as long as they were *good* stories, with the right balance of sophistication and underbelly.

"And so," I said with bated breath and painted lips, "Nigel Smith came up to you?"

"Sure did." From here, she affected a Richard Burton accent, "He said, 'I'm Nigel. Nigel Smith. I'm in from London.'" Kathy put down her blush brush. "So I said, 'Well, I'm Kathy Smith. *Kathleen* Smith. That's right. I'm Irish, buddy boy. And our two sides don't have the best history.'"

Kathy was never much for reading so I doubt she knew what the history between England and Ireland was, but just from overhearing so many older Irish relatives lament the homeland's subjugation under British rule, she could tell it wasn't any too damn good. She said she tried to take Nigel Smith to task for how the British drove Grampa Barney out of County Cavan in the 1920s—even though, in truth, it was the IRA that did it when they said, "You're either with us or against us, Bernard Smith," causing Grampa Barney to set sail for Ellis Island and board a train to a relative's tenement in Chicago. No such technicalities matter when you're three deep in your cups at Haggerty's, though. What mattered was that Nigel Smith liked Kathy Smith's moxie and asked her out.

Just picturing the scene where Kathy wrote her number on a cocktail napkin and handed it to Nigel Smith was enough to cast my eyes aloft to the cobwebbed corners of her bedroom ceiling, as though a choir of angels had just announced a shipment of my favorite mint-flavored Girl Scout cookies. "You mean…I could have a British brother-in-law?" The way my eyes gaped, you'd think Nigel Smith were on one knee before me instead of my sister.

"We're not there yet," she shook her head at every word, "Let's just see how it all plays out." She blotted her lips on some Puffs tissues and took a slug from her Miller can. "He's coming over in an hour to pick me up. Don't embarrass me. And, for Chrissake, take that makeup off!"

As I rubbed the makeup off my face, Kathy kept pulling clothes out of her closet and asking me what I thought she should wear. True, she deep-sixed my every suggestion but she also said, "Kyle, I love that we can talk this way. People say to me, 'You tell your little brother about your dates?' And I say, 'Yeah.' And they say, 'Isn't he, like, 10?' And I say, 'Yeah. But sometimes he says things that are so wise, you'd think he's our age. Like, after I told him I was dumping Dave…Kyle said, 'Kathy, there are other fish in the sea.' That one, Kyle, *that* one I took to heart. I said to my friends, 'That Kyle, he's one wise kid.'"

I flushed, doing all I could to fight back tears of validation. I couldn't remember Kathy ever having paid anyone a compliment, least of all me, and now she'd said this? Yet no sooner had she commended me than she reprised her earlier rant, "Don't you dare embarrass me tonight. And I gotta tell Mom not to embarrass me either. It's like you said, Channel 11's coming over. You gotta be on your best behavior."

Mom had cleared the kitchen table and thrown out all the outdated newspapers that had been rotting and yellowing on the outer-right kitchen chair since the last mayoral race. She'd Aqua-Netted her hair into a Margaret Thatcher bouffant, set out potpourri in every first-floor room and, as an added bonus, pressed play on a Makem & Clancy tape, which she had somehow reasoned—in her *Through-Looking-Glass* foreign policy—would help set the right mood for an Englishman.

Upstairs, Kathy had talked about Nigel Smith as someone she could take or leave. Yet as the minute hand ticked down to their date, she tripped all over herself to forage out the exact right outfit. Ultimately, she elected to forego the off-the-shoulder white leotard shirt that said in bold, black letters, "DRAWKCAB," which is "BACKWARD," spelled backward, so it'd look like BACKWARD-spelled-forward when viewed in a mirror. In the end, Kathy feared Nigel wouldn't get the joke (just like nobody else did) so instead she went with a mauve Joan Collins dress suit that she'd picked up with her employee discount at work. "Call me from the bottom of the stairs when he gets here," she said, "I wanna do that Gloria Swanson thing, y'know, where you slink down the rail. Does this look okay? I think we're having lobster."

Through the white lace curtain on our front-door window, which Mom had had cut from an on-sale bolt at Minnesota Fabrics before she tailored it and stitched it together herself on her Singer sewing machine, I spied a red Jaguar pulling up to the curb. A svelte man in a plum-colored, form-fitting Steve McQueen leather jacket exited the vehicle and swaggered up our walkway to the rebel dirges of Makem & Clancy. I creased down the blue Shetland wool sweater I'd gotten for Christmas and noticed that my mother was adjusting her gray Aran wool cardigan. She'd even reached inside her wool turtleneck's collar and pulled out her emerald Celtic Cross pendant, which she let dangle with pride at her throat. The doorbell rang and I made a dive for the knob.

There he was. Nigel Smith. Coruscating sea-green eyes, black hair pomaded back. My eyes drank up the sight of his leather jacket, my nose thrilled at his eau de cologne. He smiled, descended to his haunches and held out his hand to me, "Allo, I'm Nigel. Who might you be?"

I forever missed my cue to call Kathy from the bottom of the stairs. I said nothing. How could I manage a peep or a squeal, with my destiny seeming so close at hand?

"Oh, this is my youngest Kyle," said Mom, stepping up to show Nigel in, "I'm Maureen Smith."

"Oh, how do you do, Mrs. Smith? I'm Nigel Smith."

Somewhere in the game, Dad turned up, "You mean, we don't have enough Smiths in this house already?"

I gnashed my teeth at Dad in his Fruit of the Loom undershirt, stretched over his spare tire, blundering up this magnificent transatlantic exchange with his Midwest prosaicness. I turned around to sneer but noticed that three or four other members of the Smith clan had gathered around too. I wanted to say, "Don't look at them, Nigel. Just…just don't. They're…they're not attractive. Keep your eyes on me, Nigel. On me."

"Yes, yes. *Smith*," Nigel chortled, "There are a few of us in the world, aren't there?"

Dad trumpeted, "Yeah, but we're the *Irish* Smiths."

I bit down hard on my back molars. Mom shot Dad a harridan's glare and he turned and left the room. "I'll go fetch Kathleen," Mom cooed and went to do what Kathy had originally assigned me to do. How could I move from the moonlight pouring in through the front door, though, now that I had Nigel Smith there hanging the moon for me?

As soon as she heard Makem & Clancy striking up "Danny Boy," Kathy ditched her Gloria Swanson plans, booked it down the stairs and hustled Nigel out to his car. I don't think it was due to the song's political implications so much as it never failed to make her mascara run.

As Nigel started up his Jaguar, I went to my room and dreamed of the date they were going on. I'd already set my heart on a whole lifetime of visits from Nigel Smith. I hoped to speak to him over a set of Mom's Waterford crystal glasses—to smile and cajole just like I'd seen so many characters do on dates in movies—and to hear his English accent ringing ever-so-daintily off each Waterford crystal rim.

The next morning, I banged on Kathy's door and threw it open.

"How was it?" I said, panting.

"Jesus," she said, seated in her robe on her bed, "A little privacy."

"No," I roared with a force rarely mustered by a 10-year-old. Even Kathy, who could have driven all the Black-and-Tans out of Ireland with the way she'd flare her eyes, was taken aback.

"He's married," she said, "Alright? He's married. That's the end of him."

"He's married?" I shrieked.

Kathy let her head hang down.

"And he's going on dates?" I said.

Kathy gave a long, world-weary nod.

"But…but…that's a sin!"

Kathy walked over to her makeup table and started putting away her war-paint, "It's a different religion over there." She picked up a Miller can, shook it around, and, hearing no splashes, said, "Hey, wanna grab me another?"

I stepped out and closed the door. I did go and bring Kathy a Miller Lite but I didn't hang around her room. I just went back to my own bedroom and grieved.

Another week went by and, though my heart felt heavier than the largest stones on the Connemara coast, I muddled through day by day. That is until one night when Mom and Dad had gone to a church banquet. I was on the porch with my brother Keith, watching a Beatles celebration that came on PBS. I can't remember what song they were on. It'd be too perfect to say they were playing "Yesterday" and I was tearing up over all that I had lost. I do remember that I liked their Liverpudlian accents and I also remember that their featured interviews were beginning to bring back too many memories of Nigel—even though I'd only met him once.

What I remember most was Kathy tearing into the room. "Guys!" she said, "He's coming over."

"Who?"

"Nigel."

"Nigel!" I vaulted off our couch.

"Yeah, he says he wants to talk. But I don't want to talk to him. So when he gets here, just tell him I'm not home, okay?"

Kathy rumbled back upstairs. I bolted to the bathroom and ran a wet comb through my hair. Minutes later, I heard a car idling in front of our house. It took time but, in time, I heard the engine turn off. Nigel's surefooted footfalls followed soon thereafter. Keith and I both dashed over to answer the door.

"Allo, Kyle," said Nigel, "Oh, and I see here we have another brother?"

"Keith," said Keith.

"Pleased to meet you, Keith," said Nigel, "Is Kathy home?"

"No," said Keith.

"No," I repeated, wanting to add, "Oh, but I am, Nigel. *I* am."

"I see her light's on."

I said, "Yeah, um. She told us to tell you she's not home."

Keith swatted me.

Nigel nodded as he produced a thick book from inside his leather jacket, a book that had been on our own shelves for many a long year but whose spine, to my knowledge, nobody had ever cracked—*Trinity* by Leon Uris.

Nigel put his hand on my shoulder, "Give this to her. Would you, Kyle? Tell her it's from me. And tell her I'd like to see her before I head off to London."

"Oh, Nigel," I said, clutching Uris's book to my heart, "I will."

Nigel smiled, chucked my cheekbone lightly with his knuckles and walked back to his Jaguar. I watched with doleful eyes as he turned on the engine and whisked away toward the expressway.

My knees about to give way, I was piqued by the sound of Kathy bounding down the stairs, grinning as fiendishly as the Cheshire Cat, "What'd he say?"

Keith sized up our sister and huffed, "He looked hurt. And sad. But he says he wants to see you again before he goes, so call him."

I walked up to Kathy and shoved *Trinity* into her hands. "See if I ever talk to you again!"

I covered my face and ran blubbering back to my room.

From a distance, I could hear Kathy crack open a beer can.

Never again would Kathy call Nigel Smith.

Never will I forget his Protestant adulterer's figure darkening our doorway.

And never again would I let Kathy do my makeup.

THE BIGGEST WEIRDO

(*Kyle's epic meltdown in the kitchen, comparable only to that scene in* Rebel Without A Cause *where James Dean catches his father wearing his mother's apron*)

KYLE: I tried, Julius! I tried! You should have seen my attempts at normalcy—to be conventional by day for the sake of making a living. But I was like The Wolfman. The real me, the real me would take over. I feel like . . . like William Blake. *William Blake*! Which, I know, sounds great, hundreds of years later . . . but at the time! At the time! He was the biggest weirdo on the block!

JULIUS: Well, I doubt you're the biggest weirdo on Third Street. You're bucking up against some stiff competition for that title. But, Kyle, as someone who has to act normal for a great portion of the day, I can tell you, it takes a lot out of you. Ask anyone who has to do it: it takes a toll on your soul. So, that's what makes you so important to me. At the end of the day, I can be myself around you. I can be the part of me that that scrubbed-up world out there doesn't see. I . . . I count on you for my sanity.

KYLE: You count on *me* for your sanity? What are you, some kinda freak or something?

A NAME I WILL NEVER FORGET

Before Julius, I'd dated a guy who was also named Kyle. He was a fringe theater actor. We met online. His username was SophiaLoRent.

COMPLIANCE

(*Vet's office*)

ASSISTANT: And here's Marquez's medicine.

JULIUS: Is this cap childproof?

ASSISTANT: Um, (*inspects*) I don't believe so.

KYLE: What does it matter?

JULIUS: It matters.

KYLE: But we don't have kids.

JULIUS: We have cats.

KYLE: But they don't have thumbs.

JULIUS: There is still a regulatory standard to uphold at home. (*To assistant*) Is it possible to get a childproof cap?

ASSISTANT: Right away, sir.

THAT'S AMORE! DELLE PALLE!

When people ask about our trip to Rome, I don't wax on about Ostia Antica, the Colosseum or the Sistine Chapel. If they want to hear about all that, I just set them up with links to a few travel sites and maybe the *Lonely Planet* guidebook, which are far more informative than I could ever be. Instead, I talk about an incident that occurred on our last night in the Caput Mundi, something that will loom larger in my traveling memories than Capitoline Hill does over the Forum.

    A few months after we were married on our rooftop in Brooklyn (on October 15, 2011, shortly after same-sex marriage became legal in the state of New York), Julius and I went on an unofficial honeymoon. I say "unofficial" because Julius wanted our actual honeymoon to take place somewhere more exotic like Bhutan or Mali. But failing that, our frequent flier miles took us to Rome for ten days.

    Your friends aren't lying when they tell you about the grandeur of the Roman ruins and the wonderland of the bustling piazzas, but that said, we weren't bowled over by the service in the restaurants. The staff seemed to keep their eyes on one thing and one thing only: table-turnover. No smiles, no small talk, no getting-to-know-you. Just eat it, pay for it and *vattene via!* They left the charm to the Bernini fountains outside. At first, we just took it for what it was, but on our second to last night there, we couldn't take the impersonality anymore and absolutely RIPPED this one trattoria on TripAdvisor (they brought us the wrong entrees *twice* and copped an attitude each time we told them so) and were gratified to see that people were replying with thank you's, saying they wouldn't dare patronize said establishment after reading our review.

So, on our last night, we were wary as we'd set out to find a place that our friend Ed had recommended. Turns out, that place was closed. But there was this one quaint pizzeria that seemed to be open one street away, near the Campo di Fiori.

To protect the innocent and the guilty, we'll call this place Grazioso Ristorante. As we went up to read the menu that Grazioso had posted in a glass case on an olive vine-entwined gas lamp outside, the olive-skinned waiter stepped out with open arms, saying in English, "Come in! Come in!" This was such a contrast to what we'd experienced in other restaurants that we couldn't but comply. He pulled out our chairs and, when we sat down, he damn near fanned out our napkins and laid them in our laps.

He took one look at my unalterable pallor and said, "You must be from Ireland." I said, no, my grandparents were but I'm from Chicago and I live in New York. He replied, "Really? I mean, you're tall. You're so light-skinned. I thought, oh, he's Irish for sure." He said his best friend is from County Cork. He mentioned another best friend in Boston. Oh, and another best friend in Macedonia. If memory serves, the best of his best friends lives in Spain. Anyway, you get the picture: the guy speaks English (in a cascading Mediterranean accent), has best friends all over the place and, given the fanfare he gave us at the door, I can't say I was surprised.

He told us his name is Billy (short for Guglielmo, anglicized) and he asked where we were staying. Julius said, "We rented an apartment on Vicolo delle Palle."

Billy laughed. He leaned in and whispered, "You know what *le palle* means, don't you? *Palle* means… balls."

Apparently, our sublet was located on a cobblestone strip where butchers from time out of mind gelded rams and lambs and bulls.

We all tittered over this like schoolboys as we ordered our Margherita pizzas and Chiantis. Billy kept coming by before and after he brought out our orders. He asked about New York and about what we'd seen in Rome and of the world. Somehow we got on the topic of Poland and I said I'd been to Cracow and I'd also grown up in a largely Polish neighborhood in Chicago. Julius mentioned that our cleaning lady Irena is from Poland.

Billy cocked his head, "You live together?"

Julius and I knitted our brows.

I said, "Well, yeah, I mean, what are you missing here, Billy?"

Julius added, "We're married."

Evidently, this was a game-changer. Now Billy's inviting us out on the town. Somewhere in his thirties, with a strapping bod and a smile that undoubtedly had greased the portals to every hotspot on the Tiber, we sensed that Billy was a one-way ticket to us missing our flight the next morning. So we said we couldn't go, we had to pack and be up early. Billy simulated a tear running from the corner of his eye and walked off to get our check. He returned with complimentary glasses of port. We told him he didn't have to. He said it was his pleasure. We paid, he came back with change, said he'd say goodbye when we're done with our port and went to look after other tables.

I turned to Julius, "You know what? Let's leave Billy an extra big tip. And let's give Grazioso Ristorante five stars on TripAdvisor. Oh, I know it's nothing Michelin-starred, but what I pay for is hospitality – and Billy knows just how to make a guy feel comfortable."

I took another sip of port and got up to go to the bathroom. I saw Billy and asked him where it was. Billy told me to follow him. He came to the entrance of an empty banquet hall, looked both ways, pointed toward a corridor and said with glinting eyes, "It's over there."

I said, "Thank you."

With that, Billy cupped one hand on my ass and one hand on my *palle*.

Somehow I didn't see this coming. What did he want me to do? Turn and cough? My face looked like the cover of *Home Alone*.

As I booked it into the john and barricaded myself behind the door, it occurred to me that, if this had been the 70s or 80s, this moment might have turned out differently. I saw *Boys in the Band* and *Torch Song Trilogy*. I've read all about the baths and the loading-dock trysts of yore. In the grab-it-while-it's-hot spirit of those times, I might not have been such a stone monogamist. I might have gone in with Billy, not caring that somebody was out there waiting for me. "He'd do it too" might have been the street logic.

But here and now, it wasn't just anybody who was out there waiting for me. It was my husband, and Bacchus only knows where Billy and his best friends had been (something else I might not have considered, had this been the 70s). So, I went ahead and, *tutto solo*, did what I'd gone in there to do. But let me tell you, it was some time before urine felt free to flow.

No fool Billy. Right when I'd shut and locked the door behind me, he'd made a beeline back to our table to talk to Julius, as though rushing to his alibi. (His unspoken defense must have read something like, *"I was-a here with you-a the whole-a time-a, no? Whatever-a your husband is-a about to-a tell you-a happened, didn't-a happen. The whole time, I was-a here with you-a, amico. Capisce?"*)

I came back to our table and Billy extended his hand to me—open, not cupped, this time: "Oh, my friend! So good to meet you." I shook his hand, giving him a knowing eye as Julius and I made our way out of Grazioso Ristorante and onward to Vicolo delle Palle.

Before the door banged shut behind us, I whispered to Julius, "He grabbed my balls, Julius. *Billy. Grabbed. My. Balls.*"

Julius chuckled, "I thought he would."

This…is what I married.

For the rest of the night, until we were all packed and in bed, Julius smiled and peacocked around the Vicolo delle Palle apartment, as though Billy had just reaffirmed for him his own good taste. After all, nothing says good taste like grabbing a customer's testicles at the pizzeria where you work.

The next morning, I flew to London to see my friend Rachael. Just back from her first battery of treatments at Royal Marsden Cancer Hospital, she was rickety and rattled and her husband Adam had told me she needed to hear funny stories so I led with the one about Billy. Normally, she'd have loved such a story. After all, she's the one who used to tell me about fancy-dress do's where grown men, who were broadcasters and barristers by day, would don primary-schoolboy uniforms, dandle each other on the knee and finger-feed each other pudding, spiked with rum, before putting each other to bed. But about Billy, she was oddly somber, "But, but…that's assault."

"In Roma," I replied, like a case-hardened Casanova, "That's amore…delle palle."

THE UNIVERSE

(*Out at dinner, Julius studies an app on his phone.*)

JULIUS: I'm just checking our investment portfolio. *(Cocks one eye up)* Don't give me that look. This is important.

KYLE: Well, I'm not worried at all. The Universe always provides.

JULIUS: Ha! The Universe!

KYLE: Yeah, the Universe.

JULIUS: The Universe doesn't feed us.

KYLE: The hell it doesn't! Where do you think this food comes from?

JULIUS: An organic farm upstate.

KYLE: I mean "comes from" in a vaster sense of "comes from."

JULIUS: Kyle, the Universe doesn't exist.

KYLE: Oh really? Then tell me, what planet are we on?

JULIUS: Well, I at least live on planet Earth.

KYLE: Well, I'm a Taurus, I'm an earth sign, so I'm right there with you. And are we among other planets that comprise a solar system?

JULIUS: Yes. I've been to the planetarium, thank you.

KYLE: Oh, good! Then maybe you can tell me, which galaxy do we live in?

JULIUS: The Milky Way.

KYLE: And are there galaxies apart from our galaxy?

JULIUS: Yes. There's Andromeda and—

KYLE: Bang! The Universe exists.

JULIUS: Maybe technically it exists. But does the Universe feed you?

KYLE: I'm eating right now, right? And I haven't missed a meal in all my life…except when my folks used to send me to bed without supper—assholes.

JULIUS: Well, okay, then. Maybe the Universe wouldn't mind picking up the check for you tonight?

KYLE: Well, let's not go crazy. I'm an artist, I need a go-between.

ISLANDERS & ALLIGATORS

After meditating from 6:30 a.m. to 11 p.m. for two weeks straight at Meditationszentrum Beatenberg in Switzerland, I herniated two discs in my lower back. As a result, I developed sciatica and had to start seeing a chiropractor twice a week.

In the physical therapist's studio of my chiropractor's office, there's a whole team of burly guys who are constantly talking about full-contact sports and other things that, let's just say, guys like me ain't exactly known for talking about much.

One particular afternoon, all of the PT team, except for my physical therapist Sean, had some downtime while I was in the studio doing exercises for my sciatica. One of the guys said, "I'm starting to think there's something to that thing where they say 'age is just a number.' I think I told ya, my uncle's girlfriend's kid won that contest to play against some of the guys from the Islanders. And some a those guys, man, they're 50, 54. And they hustled him at first. *(My ears pricked up at this point.)* Made him think he was on the ice playin' a bunch of decrepit old men. *(My ears pricked down at this point.)* They switched it up on him, though. Turned up the juice. Next thing he knows: dude's 25 years old and flat on his back. They're skatin' rings round him, bro."

One of the guys grunted, "Yeah."

I couldn't participate in this exchange to any convincing degree so I just went over metta meditation phrases in my head.

The scuttlebutt continued.

"New iPhone's gonna be a thousand bucks, bro."

Sean turned away from me for a second and weighed in, "What? They gonna let you shoot an 8-millimeter hollow bullet out the camera or somethin'?"

They all made a one-grunt laugh in unison and circled away on separate walks round the studio, checking on the weights and equipment.

Gizmos and gadgets have never really been my thing—I still do most of my writing with a Bic pen and a spiral notebook—and there wasn't much of an opening for a discussion of Proust, so I stayed quiet.

Further bull-shooting ensued among the guys but Sean and I were busy working on the squats I've had to do every day at home to strengthen my discs. Bless Sean's soul, he's so patient with me. I would have thrown in the towel on me at least two sessions before this one. I never could seem to get the squats right.

Sean said, "Kyle, I know. It's not how people usually do these things. But you have to make a conscious effort. You can't just drop your knees like James Brown at show's finale. You gotta stick your butt out. You gotta stick it out more than you even think is reasonable. There's no more delicate way to put it. You gotta stick your butt

OUT! Okay? Really let it hang out there. Be like powerlifters when they do squats."

Again, the reference was lost on me. I kept trying but my knees were too far forward and my ass was too far in.

Finally, Sean said, "Look. This might work. Let's try to visualize. You ever try to close the homeroom door in school when you were a kid? You know, with your butt? Like this?" And he gave a quick demo of how to close a classroom door with one's own rear end.

No, I'd never done any such thing with a homeroom door.

But suddenly I flashed on this sassy girl from back in kindergarten. Her name was Courtney and she used to wear blue jeans that had the words "See Ya Later" stitched on the left thigh and a picture of an alligator stitched on to her right back pocket.

Courtney had a thing for me. Almost every day she'd walk up to me after the last school bell and say, "Kyle!" I'd shake and tremble as she'd point to her thigh and say, "See Ya Later." Next, she'd turn herself sideways, stick her tush out to the ends of the earth, and pointing to her right back pocket, Courtney would say, "*Alligator!*"

I'd back away every time like I'd just seen Mary Worth in the bathroom mirror and I'd run for my life. Yet on this particular visit to the studio, it occurred to me that Courtney might have been on to something all those years ago.

As Sean and his boys stood around me, I squatted and, instead of visualizing weightlifters deadlifting 500 pounds of lead, I visualized Courtney and stuck my behind out farther that it's ever gone before. From squat to squat, I silently counted:

"One...*Alligator!*"

"Two...*Alligator!*"

Sean said, "Hey! Look at that! Attaboy!" He turned to his coworker buddies and said, "Hey, look! He's really doin' it now!"

"Seven...*Alligator!*"

"Eight...*Alligator!*"

His coworker buddies nodded along with closed mouths and raised eyebrows.

I felt like an Islander.

AN ATTRACTIVE NUISANCE

(*Phone call transcript*)

KYLE: So you're saying we're being sharked?

JULIUS: I don't know. All I know is, when I walked out to go to work this morning, there was this woman sitting on our stoop, rolling a cigarette.

KYLE: Was she homeless?

JULIUS: No. She had a nice handbag and clean clothes. She even put some tissues under herself so she wouldn't wet her pants.

KYLE: How does putting tissues under yourself keep you from wetting your pants?

JULIUS: You know what I mean: Getting her pants wet.

KYLE: Well, why didn't you say that then?—So what'd you say to her?

JULIUS: I said, "What are you doing?" She said, "I'm rolling a cigarette." I said, "But you don't live here." She said, "We all live somewhere."

KYLE: Did you tell her that's a straw-man argument?

JULIUS: I did. But she said, "What's a straw-man argument?" So, I started giving her examples but she kept acting like she didn't know what I was talking about.

KYLE: Yeah, people who make straw-man arguments do that a lot.

JULIUS: I know. And I had to get to work. So she lights up the cigarette she just rolled. I said, "I don't want you doing that here." And she said, "Fine," and moved along.

KYLE: So why do you think she's staking out our place?

JULIUS: Because I've seen this kind of thing before. They keep an eye out. Or she might climb on to our stoop, fall down and try suing us for the insurance money.

KYLE: But she was trespassing.

JULIUS: It doesn't matter. She could make a lot of noise and make an attractive nuisance.

KYLE: Was she attractive?

JULIUS: Are you kidding? No! I mean, she could've been, but she went way too heavy on the compact and her rouge was rubbish. But you don't have to be attractive to create an attractive nuisance. You just have to say, "Oh, I was tired! And I saw this beautiful garden! And I just wanted to sit down and smoke a cigarette, but they have faulty stairs so I fell and I may never walk again."

KYLE: Well, why didn't she go to Geoff and Jeff's place down the street? They have a beautiful garden now.

JULIUS: But. Not. Like. Ours.

KYLE: You'll never forgive them for getting our gardeners' card, will you?

PROFUNDITY

For the past few days, I've been on my own in Geneva, Switzerland.

On the plaza where I'm writing, a swarthy man with a palsied leg and a tattered paper cup walks from table to table on a forearm crutch begging for coins. I was deep into writing by the time he leaned on my table, casting his shadow over my notebook. I smiled up at him, deposited some francs into his cup and went back to writing. Still, he hovered.

I tried to keep writing but he wouldn't move.

I took out my ear-buds.

"*Vous écrivez beaucoup,*" he said, "*Si couramment. Vous êtes très intelligent.*"

"*Merci, monsieur,*" I said, "*Je dois continuer.*"

I smiled, nodded and put my ear-buds back in. He hobbled over to another table.

He didn't need to compliment me. After all, I'd already given him money. Yet he felt compelled to express his admiration for how I was writing. I'm not sure he would have done this if he'd known *what* I had been writing:

> I fear split ends now that I've switched
> to the hotel's shampoo. My usual Prell

is bound to have different ingredients from the Swiss companies. Tomorrow I am going on a two-week Buddhist meditation retreat in Beatenberg, though. Maybe it's best that I get my head shaved before Saturday. No split ends that way, and it might make me appear to be a more dedicated practitioner. But how do you tell a barber, "Shave my head?" in French, and will he do it? Of course he'll do it. They don't sue each other as much as we Americans do.

DELUSIONS OF GRANDEUR

KYLE: And here I am, 41 years old. It wasn't well-planned. I said I wanted to be a writer. But I looked to Mick Jagger. An early 1970s Mick Jagger no less. I saw myself reading short stories to sold-out stadiums while wearing a crosshatched bolero jacket and glittering silver eye shadow—after narrowly escaping the paparazzi. The hordes swelled and swooned. I had (*huffs*) delusions of grandeur.

JULIUS: We've all had delusions of grandeur at one point or another. You know how I thought I'd die?

KYLE: How?

JULIUS: I thought I'd be at an ambassador's ball, wearing a Tuxedo under an assumed name so my adversary wouldn't find me.

KYLE: Who's your adversary?

JULIUS: I don't know. But some Judas would tell him I'm attending the ambassador's ball. And as I'm climbing the marble staircase in my Tuxedo, he's standing behind a tree in the garden. He raises a high-capacity assault rifle, gets me in his crosshairs and fires five times. And I'd put my hand over each bullet hole and tumble in slow motion down each stair to the landing.

KYLE: Jesus! Banks *really* don't like compliance officers, do they?

JULIUS: My point is we all have delusions of grandeur at a tender age—

KYLE: I was thirty.

JULIUS: Well, maybe it's time to look to more attainable horizons. Like, who was that Scottish woman on YouTube? You know, around the time Obama first took office?

KYLE: Susan Boyle?

JULIUS: Yes. Remember how she shook off that moo-moo when her ship came in?

ZERO DARK SQUIRRELLY:
COCKLOFT, PART II

The Staten Island Blutos fucked up.

The squirrel came back.

Not a sound could be heard in our library on that subzero January morning. Nothing except for the howling of arctic wind through the open windows and the growling of a squirrel who had clawed its way up the saffron-colored drapes. Now it was perched on the chestnut curtain rod, threatening to pounce.

Julius and I stood post.

We were carrying broomsticks.

We were wearing snow pants, ski gloves, winter coats, winter hats, long johns, and snow boots.

We didn't want to kill it.

We just wanted the little fucker out.

It had been terrorizing us all weekend.

We'd left all our library windows open to facilitate its escape—all except for the one right below where the squirrel was perched—the potentially rabid squirrel.

If only there were some way to rout it over to one of the other windows. That way, we could run it out and it could jump from the second-floor sill to one of the long, gangly branches of the elm tree by the curb. Yet it stayed perched and growling above the closed window, which neither one of us made a move to open, lest the beast attack.

For all their bluster and reassurances, the Animal Care and Control guys had failed to seal up the upper right-hand corner of the cockloft. The squirrel, fondly remembering the grapes and dates and oranges and persimmons in the bowls on our kitchen countertops, had wended its way back into our house. We called in the animal-control guys again. They copped to their error, sealed up the corner they'd missed, said have a nice day and packed up to head back to Staten Island.

"But what about the squirrel?" I said to the foreman and his assistant.

Julius said, "It's still in the house."

"We hear him in the walls at night," I said. "Have you ever heard a squirrel in the walls? In the middle of the night? Trust me, it's scarier than any nightmare you could possibly dream up. The creeping. The scratching. The hovering. The...the *scratching!* And you never know where it is at any moment. You only know that the sound is coming from inside the walls."

"I know how squirrels-in-the-walls sound," said the foreman, "It's been my business for the past 30 years."

"Well, if you know so much, get him out of here!" Julius said.

"There's only so much I can do," said the foreman, "He's your problem now."

"Oh thanks" said Julius.

"Have a nice day," said the foreman as he made his way to the door with his adjustable ladder and with the assistant who'd fucked up the sealing the first time.

"I'm gonna call your supervisor," Julius said to the foreman.

"You're looking at him," said the foreman. "Have a nice day."

For the next three mornings, we'd walk downstairs to the kitchen, red-eyed and grim from a long night of hearing the squirrel scraping out its dominion on the insides of our walls. Former rescue kittens, now senior cats who've grown all-too-used to the good life, Marquez and Giuseppe would greet us in close proximity to their food bowls with spooked eyes and fluffy tails as they stationed themselves on countertops and tables where they'd reasoned that the vermin—whom nature had designed them both to kill—would be more likely to leave them in peace. The pieces of fruit in our bowls were ravaged, little tooth and claw marks visible in the rinds. Plants and lamps were kicked over in the squirrel's wake. Amid the disrepair and the squirrel's disregard for our property, Julius and I had even begun snapping at each other. In a matter of several short days, the squirrel had managed to make utter chaos of our lives.

"I don't kill animals," Julius told me, "But this thing is scratching up my stenciled Oriental Peacock wallpaper and ripping up the taffeta tablecloth. If Marquez and Giuseppe aren't gonna take him out, I will."

And now at last we had it cornered. We'd spotted its sorry ass in the hallway. Both the cats had seen it and both of them had jumped on to the bannister, where they now stood quivering. The squirrel had even turned to look up and chirp and taunt them. That is, until we stepped in. This time, the squirrel sensed we meant business. It charged into the library and we slammed the door behind it to keep it contained as we decamped to change into protective clothing for a final showdown.

By 7:03 a.m., we'd entered the library with broomsticks and wintertime battle fatigues.

Monday, January 21, 2013.

Martin Luther King Jr. Day.

Also, the day of the Second Inauguration of President Barack Obama.

If we could pull this off, we'd be free at last.

Now the squirrel was roaring, its claws clicking as it paced back and forth on the curtain rod.

"If I push it off with this," I said, pointing to the broomstick, "Then maybe it'll jump to the floor, hang a right and lemming-dive out the window."

"If you push it off the curtain rod," Julius said, "It will dive straight into your face, scratch your boyish cheeks to bloody ribbons and gnaw your nose off like that guy in *Silence of the Lambs*."

"Well, it's freezing in here," I said, "How long are we going to let it hold us hostage?"

"Hostage?" said Julius, "That's not the way he sees it. He thinks he's the hostage."

"Well, how can he be the hostage when we've left the windows wide open for him? Hostage-takers, by definition, hold hostages captive, whereas we stand in complete support of this squirrel's freedom."

"The way he sees it," said Julius, "We're the ones holding broomsticks. In his mind, it's kill-or-be-killed."

"If only there were some way to explain," I said, "And here it is, your day off. We were going to watch the inauguration."

"We can still watch the inauguration."

"No we can't," I said, "Even if we turn the TV on in here, our eyes are still gonna be on this goddamn squirrel."

The squirrel was now cawing and moaning.

"The inauguration isn't 'til noon."

"But this thing can hold out as long as we can," I said, "We might be in here all day with this little fucker."

Right as I said this, our neighbor Nicola and her husband Andrew were walking their standard poodle right in front of our house. "Oh my God," I cheered, spotting them outside the window, "There's Nicola!"

Julius knew that, when I'd posted word of the squirrel's first visit on Facebook, Nicola had commented, "If you ever have that problem again, let me know. I'm from Corpus Christi. I have lots of experience removing critters from houses."

Why hadn't I thought of this before?

Julius dashed over to one of the open windows and shouted in his best Stanley Kowalski, "Hey,

Nicccccooooolaaaaa!," which alone made the squirrel shudder and moan.

Having gotten her attention, he explained the situation loud enough for the whole block to hear. Nicola handed her standard poodle's leash over to Andrew and let him take over the walk as she took a sip out of her Starbucks canteen and strode past our gate and up our stairs. The squirrel and I stared each other down, unblinking, as Julius let Nicola in.

Nicola stepped into the library. Julius closed the door behind her. The squirrel was now baying like the Hound of the Baskervilles.

"Hi, Nicola," I said, "Now what?"

Nicola shrugged, "I just try to scare it."

"Okay," I said, nodding, "That much has been accomplished."

"Why don't you just open up that window?" Nicola said.

"Because I'd like to still have a face when this is all over."

"Do you want me to open it?" she said.

"What if it jumps down?" Julius chimed in.

Nicola walked over to the window, "I don't care if a squirrel falls on my head."

"How can you not care if a squirrel falls on your head?"

Unfastening the window lock, Nicola simply answered, as calm as daybreak, "I'm from Texas."

Nicola opened the window. A new blast of cold air rushed in. As Nicola took a few steps over to the couch, I saw behind her what looked like the bottom of a bearskin rug falling through the now-open window with the ease of a sheet of rainwater washing down a pane of glass. Julius and I took a moment to marvel at the spectacle of the squirrel's descent and then bolted over to slam the windows shut.

We each scooped Nicola into our arms and spun her around as wildly as the crowded curio shop that we call our library would allow.

The cockloft was sealed.

The squirrel was gone.

Not only did we get to see Barack Obama getting sworn in to a second term on CNN but we guzzled two whole bottles of champagne, left over from the holiday season, as we did it.

The ordeal was over.

We were no longer under siege.

A few weeks later, we went to Nicola's house with a present that we'd ordered for her from an online store called Road Kill Cafe. It was a black t-shirt featuring a squirrel holding up a mug-shot board. The caption read: "It's All Fun and Games Until Someone Loses a Nut."

How well we could relate to the caption after all that we'd been through with our cockloft.

CENTER-STAGE

(In his sleep, Julius shrieks and then screams like a kettle fired up to a whistle. Kyle rustles him.)

KYLE: Julius, wake up.

JULIUS: *(coming to)* Whaa-whaa-wot?

KYLE: You're having a nightmare.

JULIUS: *(rubs his eyes)* Oh, it wasn't a nightmare. It was a beautiful dream. I was singing center-stage at La Scala and I got to wear a cape.

CASUAL COERCION

There's a "bespoke" emergency at Julius's techie office. People are encouraged to dress casually at work but management has observed that some are showing up in jeans that they don't consider à la mode. For this reason, a designer has been called in to take the measurements of anyone who "would like" a more *au courant* sort of denim. All staff members are strongly encouraged to attend this meeting.

7 MISSISSIPPI

JULIUS: Great! The Wi-Fi went out again.

KYLE: I'll reset it.

JULIUS: Turn it off a total of 10 seconds.

KYLE: (*Kyle switches off box*) 10 Mississippi, 9 Mississippi, 8 Mississippi . . . Wait, what comes after 8 Mississippi?

JULIUS: You have GOT to be kidding me.

KYLE: Well, shit, I was an English major.

LE JOURNAL D'UNE FEMME DE CHAMBRE—MONTRÉAL

(*Translated from the French*)
8 April 2017

From what I could make out, the peculiar American with the snow-white skin was asking his partner (the one who spoke French to me in what seemed a heavy Puerto Rican accent), "So how about my butt?"

I believe this American's name was Kyle. He was standing by the bed and had been asking his partner to compartmentalize him from top to bottom throughout the time I spent cleaning the sink. He'd flattened out the woolen midriff of his sweater and looked at himself sideways in the full-length mirror, until at last he inquired of his Puerto Rican mate, who had the same first name as a distinguished Roman emperor:

I just want to know, if this were the 1970s and you were a teenage girl, would you think I was a rock star? And would you target me for a paternity suit?

Who asks such questions?
But I do not ask questions. I simply clean and take notes.

(*signed*)
La Femme de Chambre

CUTPURSE

(*As the sun sets over Brooklyn, Kyle walks home from Flatbush Avenue—one step behind a short woman, who keeps shooting looks back at him like he's a mugger or something worse. Kyle has finally had enough . . .*)

KYLE: Oh puh-leeze, lady. I'm a gay man carrying a Kindle full of modernist novels. What could I possibly want with your purse? (*Beat*) Actually, now that I've heard myself put it that way . . . let me just get a couple steps ahead of you here and we'll call it a night.

WIDE-EYED

My mother, who was my own personal Phyllis Schlafly growing up, wanted to buy my nephew Sean a pair of Nikes for his birthday. She saw they were on sale at Dick's Sporting Goods. "So, I went on the Internet," she told me, "And I typed in DICKS. Oh, Kyle! You should have seen what came up on the screen!" What could I do but nod.

THE MANDARINS

(*At Sartre/Beauvoir's grave, Montparnasse Cemetery, Paris*)

KYLE: (*on one knee, clasps heart*) Simone, I'm back.

BEAUVOIR: *Oui. Je vois. Mais*…Have you returned to me as a bestselling author?

KYLE: A'right, Simone. We're done here.

(*Kyle gets off knee. Exits.*)

SARTRE: (*to Beauvoir*) Yet another smitten writer you've thrown to the wolves.

BEAUVOIR: (*to Sartre*) You're a fine one to talk.

PARIS BIRTHDAY

(*41st birthday dinner in Paris*)

JULIUS: (*raises glass*) To you.

KYLE: (*clinks*) A birthday dinner at Taillevent. This is almost as romantic as that time the waiter groped me in Rome.

JULIUS: You thought that was romantic?

KYLE: No, what was romantic was what you said when we were in bed later: "Well, if I was waiting your table, I would've groped you too."

JULIUS: And I would have.

KYLE: Even if I wasn't seated in your section?

JULIUS: I would have moved you to my section.

KYLE: Awww . . . Y'know, how come it's only when we're in Europe that you turn into this silver-tongued devil, you?

"IS THIS ONE OF THOSE BUDDHIST MEDITATIONS?"

February 5, 2013

I just flew in to Chicago to see my mom. She turned 80 on Friday. Five years ago, she was diagnosed with ovarian cancer and was given five years to live. Now my dad is telling me, "I hope you have a suit and tie back in New York. You're gonna have to come back wearing it pretty soon."

From her first chemo treatment on, I had not seen Mom's real hair. I'd only seen her in wigs, sometimes a red one, sometimes brown, sometimes a silver gray, which was a bold choice for a woman who had always colored her hair, never letting a single root show, right up to the day of her diagnosis. As she stands at the door to greet me, though, all disguises are off. A shock of pure white hair stands on end off her head. Several bald patches show. For much of her life, Mom was full-figured. Now she is a skeleton with a sallow coat of melted wax hanging off her. Even at her sickest, she always used to have her makeup on and at least a wool cardigan and a pair of slacks. Now she spends all day in the same green bed-gown and, given how much time she has to stay in bed, there's no point in putting on makeup every morning if it's just going to end up smeared across her face when she falls asleep a couple hours after waking up.

Years ago, my friend Ruth said my mother reminded her of Jackie O. I didn't quite see why until Mom got cancer. From the time of the Kennedy assassination until her final years, Jackie seldom, if ever, complained and neither has Mom. Jackie put a high premium on comportment and so does Mom. But now Mom doesn't have the energy for dressing up and I suspect she no longer wants to hide what is happening to her, much like Jackie when she refused to change the pink suit that was spattered with her husband's blood and brains.

Mom and I walk into her living room and talk. My siblings and I all grew up in the city but my parents moved to a suburb 10 miles or so north of Chicago once we were all moved out, so their current house was never my home. It was just a place I'd visit every now and then. Now it smells like my grandparents' home did in their waning years—that musty, medicine-y smell. Mom wants to hear all about my cats and asks after my husband Julius, which is a big step for her, maybe the biggest she'll ever be able to take toward accepting not only that I'm gay (out since age 17, so she's had time to get used to it), but gay-married. When she didn't even so much as call to wish me luck on my wedding day in October 2011, I didn't speak to her for the better part of a year. Now it seems silly to hold a grudge.

A lot of small talk drops from her lips as I focus on the tight skin on her forehead and cheekbones, wondering if that's how she'll appear at her wake. One of my bugaboos has been how I'll react to seeing her in an open casket. When I was little, family members would have to drag me to the caskets at wakes. The dead in them looked so lifelike, I was afraid they'd open their eyes and jump out. Now my fear is that I'll break down in a sobbing mess when Mom is up there. When you're Irish, you're allowed only a certain amount of falling-apart at a wake. Then you're supposed to pull yourself together and make a big, funny show of how life goes on. If we were Italian, this wouldn't be an issue. If I'd break down, I'd have plenty of company in crying.

Mom and I speak for another 45 minutes or so, then she has to go lie down. Dad tells me he's surprised she was able to sit up this long. If she so much as walks down the ten-foot hallway, she has to sit down and rest up for 10 or 15 minutes before proceeding into the kitchen. She can't go to Mass in the morning or on Sundays anymore, so Dad goes every day and brings back Communion.

He tells me she doesn't want her funeral to be in the church in our old neighborhood in the city. She wants it to be at the parish where they live now. She also wants to be buried with a brother of mine named Brian, who died as an infant long before I was born. Brian never had a tombstone—my parents were young and broke when they had him—but my mother has saved up to buy him one for when she is laid to rest next to him. Mom has also resolved to buy one for my father's mother, who died giving birth to him, before her bones lay next to Brian's.

    I take all this in and tell Dad I'm going to go meditate. I forget whom I'm talking to. It's too late, though, and I brace myself for the question I know is coming next, "Is this one of those Buddhist meditations?" I say yes and expect to be baited about not being a Catholic anymore, as if long time ago when I was one, it was by choice. But Dad is getting on in years and mercifully doesn't have the energy to fight with me about it anymore. As for Mom, she is just glad I believe in something. To my surprise, Dad asks if I'd like him to leave the room so I can have some privacy while I meditate. (When has any father ever asked that? So, again, subtle progress.) I say, "Thanks but I'll go to the guest room," where I'm staying.

    I fashion a meditation cushion out of a pile of pillows from the linen closet and stack them up on the bed. There's a Crucifix above the bed and a rosary on the nightstand. I see they've put a new collection of saints' statues and a vial of holy water on the desk at the foot of the bed too. This is going to be one wild meditation. My mother has lived by church rules all her life. I have not. She is sure of where she's going when she closes her eyes to this world. I envy her that.

    I set my iPhone timer for 45 minutes and get started on my metta (loving-kindness) meditation: "May I be happy/May I be at peace/May I be happy/May I live with ease…" I was relieved to learn, many years ago, that it is not selfish to wish ourselves happiness when doing metta. On the contrary, the more happiness we have, the more we have to give. So I send metta to myself for a good long time before moving on to the Benefactor, the Loved One, the Neutral Person, the Enemy and so on. As I progress through my meditation, I know I'm only at the wee small hours of beginning to integrate all that I've seen and learned since entering my parents' house. I can tell, on some level, I've steeled myself against it. As I sit, I feel like a block of ice that's only melting by degrees in the heat of meditation, though in time I know I'll be puddle when I enter the last stages of grief.

Tonight Mom says we'll watch some of the new *Downton Abbey* DVD I brought with me. Every Sunday night, Julius and I watch it over Margherita pizza. She says she'll watch as much as she can before she has to go lie down again.

I leave tomorrow afternoon for New York. The next day, I'll take my suit in to be pressed.

> (Maureen Ann Smith passed away on March 11, 2013. Thomas Philip Smith, her husband of 54 years, passed away of prostate cancer-related complications on February 11, 2014.)

WIDE-EYED, THE PREQUEL

(The year is 1995. After a period of estrangement, Kyle's mother drops by his apartment with some drapes she has sown and hopes he'll put up.)

MOM: Kyle . . . you know, I've been thinking . . . This *Kate* gal you've mentioned . . . You speak as though you're in love with her. I, I think you should make Kate your girlfriend.

KYLE: Mother, Kate is my best friend. And yet again, you're in denial about the fact that I. AM. GAY.

MOM: Well, some people like it both ways.

(Kyle's eyebrows go up. His mother puts her hand over her Celtic Cross pendant and looks down at the drapes in her arms, unable to believe what she has just said.)

MOM: Now, if you'll notice, this pattern has a slight hint of red and green paisley.

FOUNTAIN OF THE PEEING BOY IN FOOTIE PAJAMAS:
AN INTRODUCTION TO LOGIC

Logic has never been my forte, so it shocked me and everyone I knew when I got an A in my Intro to Logic course in college. As a logician would say, though, there's a valid explanation for this. Homework in this particular class was optional, so if we didn't do the assignment, there were no penalties; if we got an A on the homework, the professor would give us extra credit; and if we got all the problems wrong, we knew it wouldn't impact our grade. Plus, the professor would always encourage us to go over our errors with her or her TAs at office hours. "Learning happens by trial and error" was her motto.

Our grades were based solely on midterm and final exam scores. Having nothing better to do first thing in the morning, I would actually go to class and even do the assigned homework. I never answered a single homework problem right, but after getting a big fat F each time, I'd go to office hours and the professor or one of her TAs would walk me through each problem until I'd get each one right. True, they'd practically have to resort to sock puppets, but by the time midterms and finals rolled around, I'd end up being more than capable of doing all the deductive syllogisms necessary to pull an A.

What I'm trying to illustrate is that logic has never been second nature to me. Yet, to my amazement, I've managed to get through 40 years of life and counting even though I grew up with a mind undiluted by rational thinking.

To offer another example of my imperfect left brain and hyper-developed right brain: at the same time I was taking Intro to Logic, I was working as a clerk for a claims management office. For my first couple years there, I was unacquainted with the office computers. Mostly all I did was file medical malpractice and workers comp records all day, every day, which was fine by me since it gave my mind a chance to go off on its perennial pleasure cruises while my body followed a simple, Zen regimen of stuffing carbon copies of personal injury forms into manila folders. But every so often, as I went about my office chores, gonglike booms would sound from either side of the filing cabinets. After hearing these several times, I surmised that I was having paranormal experiences, that the Universe was communicating with me—and only me—through spooky, magical crescendos. For months on the job, I attempted to decode these communications. Was I being chosen for some epic destiny? Why else would I be hearing these dramatic surges? I later discovered that what I was hearing was the sound of my supervisors turning on their Mac PCs.

These examples are part of a longstanding pattern of absentmindedness and harebrained conclusions that started way back in my childhood. They even preceded the time that our dentist's son, Johnny Matinko, came to spend the night at our house in the spring of 1979. I was five years old and my brother Kent was nine. Johnny was a year ahead of Kent in school and Kent wanted to get in good with an upperclassman so he begged our Mom to ban his embarrassing little brother (that would be me) from joining in the good times he and Johnny were planning on having together, playing with G.I. Joe action figures and Matchbox cars. Never one to suffer silently, I howled and screamed worse than any werewolf or werewolf's victim until our Mom handed down the verdict that it was only fair that I should be able to be wherever I wanted in the house.

Kent gnashed his teeth and called me "*Brat!*" as usual. It was an insult, sure, but it wasn't a swear word so he could get away with saying it. Still, it hurt every time he said it, especially since I didn't want Kent feeling annoyed by me. His steady stream of jokes was so uproarious, I felt I just had to follow him everywhere he'd go, including to the bathroom—the one place where he could yell for Mom to finally shake me off his trail.

Who could blame me, though? Kent was the one who taught me such humdingers as:

"So, the doctor said, '*Here's my thermometer, now where did I put my pen?*'"

And:

"*Doctor, Doctor! I think I'm a goat!*"
"*How long have you felt like this?*"
"*Since I was a kid!*"

After punching out these staples of his comedic repertoire, I would double over, blinded by tears of laughter, only to straighten up and find that Kent had made a break for it. I'd sometimes have to spend hours sleuthing out where he'd gone next but most of the time I managed to find him and pester him until he'd tell me more jokes.

At first, whenever these early shoots of Kent's comic genius broke through, I'd end up wetting my pants. To put an end to this putrid habit, my parents imposed a new house rule stating that, whenever Kent made me laugh to the point of urination, I'd have to go straight to the bathroom and wash my hands after flushing. On paper, this all looks reasonable enough, but my trips to the bathroom ended up quadrupling as a result of their new ordinance and my time away from Kent meant that I was missing out on a good three-fourths of his inspired knee-slappers.

I also failed to understand why one had to pee in the bathroom, of all places. Why not pee on the sidewalk or the grass or against a brick wall? It only seemed logical that, wherever one spent a penny, a whirlpool would magically appear to flush the urine away with a whoosh.

So, with official permission to participate in the fun and frolics of Kent and Johnny's sleepover, I suited up into my sunny yellow footie pajamas, which had white padded feet and white rings at the cuffs. Kent wore his orange and blue Chicago Bears PJs while Johnny's pajamas had a white background where assorted Superheroes—Superman, Batman, Green Lantern, Aquaman—showed off their various feats of power and dexterity. Johnny's jammies alone showed how much cooler he was than us. I wanted to be around him even more than Kent. This whole affair was nothing short of thrilling for me, even though they both cold-shouldered me the whole time, hoarding their Hot Wheels cars and barricading the two-tiered Mattel highway system with their bigger bodies. The best I could do was assume the sidelines. Still, I was so excited to be with the big boys, I hardly noticed how they were ostracizing me.

As we all hunkered down with toys on our bedroom's shaggy red carpet, Johnny caught sight of the Tigger knockoff that I'd gotten for Christmas the year before. This particular orange plush-toy tiger was squat, whiskery and stationary whereas the real Tigger is lithe, bouncy and has only a few strands of whiskers shooting from both ends of his upper lip. Still, it was clearly a tiger, which is why the observation that Johnny made next struck me as not only bizarre but stupid. He turned to Kent and said, "I like your lion." A lion? I sneered as I turned to Kent, awaiting his response. Kent picked up the knockoff Tigger, shook it around in front of his face and said in a gruff cartoony voice, "Tiger. I ain't lyin'!"

Johnny merely giggled but I stood up, held my belly and gasped with laughter, gobbling up gulps of oxygen like a fish. I laughed and laughed and laughed until I could feel my bladder growing heavier than an Acme Anvil. Then I laughed harder, harder than I'd ever laughed before. Flouting what I saw as a nonsensical convention, I didn't take this as my cue to go to the toilet. Instead, in a fit of hilarity, I climbed up on top of my mattress and stood above Kent and Johnny's heads, catching my breath before unzipping my footie pajamas, lowering my Underoos crotch and chuckling myself pink as I hosed down our shaggy red carpet with a pipeline full of golden water.

Kent and Johnny Matinko couldn't help but pay attention to me now. But why weren't they laughing? They both looked at me like I was a bank robber, who'd shot the teller pointblank before turning the gun on them.

To my equal dismay, though, as the last few urine drops hit the floor, I noticed that no vortex of water had arisen, as planned, to drain the offending fluid from the carpet threads.

Hot tears streamed down Johnny Matinko's face as he screamed that he wanted to go home. He refused to sleep on any of our beds and he wouldn't even accept an offer to sleep in a sleeping bag on our basement floor. After all, our basement floor was carpeted and God knows what I might have done on it during, say, a particularly amusing episode of *The Banana Splits*. After Dr. Matinko picked Johnny up to bring him home, Kent glowered at Mom for allowing me to come along and ruin his one shot at primary-grade popularity.

As Mom knelt beside a bucket of soap and water on our bedroom's shaggy red carpet, scrubbing away and remonstrating me for this senseless act, I stood in my now zipped-up footie pajamas, scratching my chin and wondering why the hell the whirlpool never showed up on our bedroom carpet the way it always did in our toilet bowls.

R.ATTR.APAGE

(Julius and Kyle lie in bed on the morning of July 4th, 2014, lost in their iPhones.)

JULIUS: Are those tears in your eyes?

KYLE: I'm reading Walt Whitman: "Oh, I see flashing that this America is only you and me/Its power, weapons, testimony, are you and me/Its crimes, lies, thefts, defections, are you and me." It's heavy stuff. You want to hear it?

JULIUS: Maybe later. I'm reading this.

KYLE: What are you reading?

JULIUS: High school students' test scores in France.

KYLE: They publish those?

JULIUS: Yes, in *Le Monde*. I look forward to it every year. See, look at this: "Marilou Gangnon - RATTRAPAGE"—FAIL!

KYLE: This is how you celebrate Fourth of July? Looking up substandard French students?

JULIUS: Well, it's not Game Over for Marilou. It says here she can retake the verbal in September.

A Reminder to Always Take a Deep Breath Before Taking Offense

I passed a woman who was chatting with her friends on Prospect Park West.

When my back was turned, she said, "Oh my God! Look at that fluffer!"

I whipped around to say, "Oh, sure. Like you never ran out of money in college."

But I paused in time to see that she'd actually been marveling at some late-season gardenias.

ETYMOLOGY

KYLE: You're right. Etymology is a fascinating subject. And to think that all these poets were the ones who invented the language we speak today.

JULIUS: For today—a time that has no patience for poetry.

KYLE: Admittedly, a lot of the poetry that made its way into our lexicon was phallocentric. Did you know the word "vagina" comes from the Latin word for "sheath"?

JULIUS: (*mishearing*) Wait. The word "vagina" came from the Latin word for "sheep"?

HOW ARE YOU GOING TO HANDLE THE END OF THE WORLD?

(*Dinner. Credits roll on TV screen. Julius breaks down sobbing.*)

KYLE: Julius. C'mon. It's *Call the Midwife*. How are you going to handle the end of the world if you can't even take PBS?

JULIUS: It's just, the squalor. The degradation. When the nun described the workhouse howl. When she said, "The inmates are tidied away in graves."

KYLE: Well, if it makes you feel better, I read in *The Guardian* that the actresses are paid a hell of a lot to say those lines.

JULIUS: And there they are, at the site of a workhouse. And here we are—eating pizza.

KYLE: Yeah, but the pizza was late, so we got it for free.

JULIUS: Why was it late?

KYLE: The guy who answers the phone said the delivery guy was breaking up with his girlfriend by text. And then she *really* didn't like that he did it by text, so the breakup took even longer than expected. Everybody's pizzas started going cold so they fired him and gave everybody who ordered free pizzas.

JULIUS: Yet more misfortune to add to this world.

KYLE: Oh God! Julius, you can't go through life treating everything like it's the last act of *Madame Butterfly*. We're running low on Kleenex as it is.

JULIUS: But it's just like the nun said, the one who always quotes Shakespeare, "Life is but a walking shadow..." It *is*.

KYLE: Alright, alright, alright. We gotta stop winding down our weekends with this show.

JULIUS: What else is there?

KYLE: I got the new *Orange Is The New Black* DVDs. You seem to enjoy the inmates at Litchfield Correctional Facility.

JULIUS: (*mops eyes*) They are more fun than the midwives' patients.

KYLE: That's right. And they don't even tidy them away in graves until their contracts are up.—Although they do sometimes send them to max when the actors get demoted to semi-regulars.

(*Julius sobs even harder now.*)

THE SECRET LIVES OF SANTORUMITES

I used to know a woman who grew up in Montana with a June Cleaver mom whose views on sex and reproductive rights were to the right of Rick Santorum. Yet one day her mother confessed to her adult daughter over coffee that, when she had the house to herself, she loved to get naked and clean their home from top to bottom. She further revealed that many of the housewives in the area shared the same kink.

In fact, her mom told her, Mrs. Tuttle down the street would accessorize her naked housecleaning with her husband's old college football helmet. She'd put it on, charge into the next room with a sponge and bucket and tackle the floor tiles, scouring them down to the granules. Mrs. Tuttle had found such liberation in this practice, she felt she could do it all day, every day.

That is, until the morning the Sears appliance repairman showed up to fix the Tuttles' washer and dryer. Mrs. Tuttle had been upstairs scrubbing the tub in nothing but her husband's football helmet while crooning to a scratchy Debby Boone album that blared from the den. The repairman had rung the doorbell and banged on the door but somehow Mrs. Tuttle hadn't heard him through all the helmet's padding. This was a small town where people didn't lock their doors, so the repairman just let himself in, found the laundry room and got to work.

Every now and then, he'd see Mrs. Tuttle walking the halls with nothing on but her husband's helmet. She failed to see or hear him, though, until at last she heard rattling emanating from the laundry room. Forgetting herself, and forgetting to put on a robe, she charged over to see what was the matter.

There stood Mrs. Tuttle, naked as Eve but for her husband's helmet.

The repairman put the last of his tools back in his toolbox and closed its locks.

He humbly got up, picked up his toolbox and maneuvered around Mrs. Tuttle as he quickened his pace toward the door.

Mrs. Tuttle grabbed a stray towel from a shelf in the laundry room and clutched it to herself as the repairman turned the front door's knob.

Before stepping back into the world, the Sears repairman paused and hung his head as he delivered these parting words to Mrs. Tuttle: "I hope your team wins, lady."

RAINDROPS DRIP OFF IRON BARS

(*Kyle and Julius lounge on the bed after work. Strings of raindrops drip off iron bars outside window.*)

JULIUS: Did you hear from anybody today?

(*Drip*)

KYLE: No.

(*Drip*)

JULIUS: Nobody?

(*Drip*)

KYLE: No.

(*Drip*)

JULIUS: Not a soul in the world?

(*Drip*)

KYLE: No.

(*Drip.*)

JULIUS: Not a single solitary soul.

(*Julius gazes at the ceiling as the water drips off the iron bars.*)

KYLE: (*also gazing at ceiling*) Our nighttime conversations are becoming like Beckett plays. This is not good.

THE KING & I

Julius sang "Getting to Know You" as he waited in line for the men's room at intermission. One by one, the guys at the urinals zipped up and turned around to face him.

SCRUFFY ARISTOCAT

I grew up on the northwest side of Chicago and went to high school on the near south side. This meant I'd have to take the EL train 14 miles from my middle-class/upper-middle class neighborhood and through (what were at the time) low-rent areas that artists had been moving into. As I'd watch this Midwest *La Bohème* society board the train for their day jobs or art-school classes every weekday morning, my heart would swell with the feeling that I was seeing my own destiny unfold.

A lot of shit-paying jobs in and out of college ensured that I had indeed been watching my own destiny unfold. I did go on to live in some cheap places in some happening areas but when the leases would be up, I'd be priced out of those areas and into neighborhoods that I and other white artsy types had been pushed into after our pale faces had made our last neighborhood a little too safe for building-flippers and plucky Yuppies.

There was a certain glamor to living where you could get mugged on your way to or from a simple toothpaste-run but, after a while, the sounds of shoot-outs and stray dogs fighting, and stray cats mating, in the alley every night, as well as the sight of a new line of bashed-in car windows on my street every morning before work got to be too dispiriting.

So I couldn't pack up the U-Haul fast enough when a family friend let my mother know that her son had moved out of the condo they'd bought him on Sheridan Road. They asked if I'd like to live there instead at the cost of the assessments, which came to a grand total of $400 a month.

Twice I'd lived in this family's place: once in my mid-twenties before I went off and failed as a writer in Europe and New York and again in my late twenties when I was saving almost half of each paycheck to move back to New York.

Dining on Ramen noodles most nights, I might have looked, dressed and acted like a character in *Rent* but I sure as hell wasn't living like one. Sure, I was paying peanuts for this apartment but it was on the ninth floor of a 28-story high-rise that stood right on Lake Michigan. It had floor-to-ceiling windows with a north-side view of a singularly Chicago cityscape. I'd fall asleep to the sound of waves breaking on the Granville Avenue rocks. It also came fully furnished with a Murphy Bed built into the other side of the kitchen wall. And by my early-late twenties, my time in the grant-writing trenches had landed me a much better job writing for a fair-housing organization, which was good for both my conscience and my savings account as I was able to squirrel away more and more money for the comeback I was staging in New York.

In the meantime, there was love to find and online dating to do.

Aside from one actor friend who had never managed to so much as find the on-off switch on the retooled word processor that had been donated to our theater and that had sat gathering dust on his desk for a full three years, I was the least tech-savvy person I knew. Nonetheless, I did manage to go to Kinko's and scan and upload to the dating site a couple surprise Polaroid shots that were taken of me gorging at the chips-and-dips table at one of our cast parties. I'd also written and rewritten my ad to show that I could rub two brain cells together, all so I could meet the kind of guy who could do the same.

I ended up meeting a lot of cement-heads who were just out for hook-ups, though, and while I was game for that, I was also naive enough to think these crash-and-burns would lead to anything. They never did. For however tough I pretended to be, my heart was too fragile not to break when it'd all be over in the morning and no messages would be left on my answering machine and no had-a-nice-time emails would land in my inbox.

I started missing even more meals so I could save even more money so I could move to New York quicker and get away from the mood that was building up and taking over my sweet-deal apartment. After so many lonely nights and blue Mondays, I began to refer to my sweet deal in my journal as "my tomb with a view."

I still left my dating profile up, though now I was scrolling through profiles of guys in the greater New York City area as I counted down the days till I could move there and date them.

But then a guy in Chicago emailed me. He was a young oncologist named Nelson who was completing his residency downtown. "Wow!" he wrote, "Right when you're just about to give up, you find the ad you've been waiting for all along." He gave long and winding reviews of all the books I'd listed as my favorites. He said that picture of me dipping my carrot stick in the French Onion dip should be on display in galleries. I looked at his profile. Nelson had a clean-shaven head and shining emerald eyes. My heart swooned. I came clean in my intro email to him, though: "Like I said in my profile, I'm moving to New York."

He shot back, "I know. But you're here now, aren't you?"

We exchanged phone numbers and, though we had to make it quick since we were both at work, we made plans over the phone to meet in person. He told me to meet him at a chichi bistro in Andersonville.

"Oh, yeah. I know it," I said, "It's not far from my apartment."

He said, "It isn't?" He seemed astonished. I was in too much a rush to ask why, though, so I said, "No. It's really close by. I'll see you there."

"Okay," he said, "It's a nice place but there's no need to dress up."

"Um, okay," I said, screwing up my eyes, "Like I said, I know the place. I'll probably be coming right from work."

Our workplace was casual so I wore jeans and my usual rings and things to the restaurant. I had gone to

Citibank first and withdrawn more money than I'd hope to for dinner but it'd been so long since I'd had a good date that I sucked it up and crumpled the ATM receipt without so much as looking at it.

Nelson was every bit as handsome as his profile and he gave me a huge hug and kiss on the cheek when I got there.

We sat down. We both ordered the spaghetti frutti de mari and he chose a wine called Sangiovese. Nelson tasted it, approved it and after the waitress poured it for both of us, he raised his glass and said, "To you."

It's hard playing it cool when someone says that with such green eyes but I'd taken what I'd learned from actors and played coy.

Nelson said, "Wow, you're really pasty."

I gulped, "Yeah. I'm afraid my first ancestors were the last in line when they were passing out pigment."

"No, no," he said, "I like it. I've always had this thing for Irish guys, especially when they're artists."

Say that to a guy who hasn't worn shorts since he was laughed out of no-uniform day in fourth grade, you'll get him rethinking his plans to move out of town.

Nelson was of German extraction. He grew up in small-town Pennsylvania but he had a most resourceful mind, one that had made him his town librarian's special favorite. At dinner, I discovered he knew even the minor works of August Strindberg as well as Ingmar Bergman's variations on them.

Nelson shared with me how his mother and father used to go on long walks together each and every night and how, the one night his mother had decided to stay home because she was tired, Nelson's dad had gone out walking on his own and was killed by a hit-and-run driver. I gasped. Nelson put his hand over mine, closed his eyes and shook his head.

Nelson sighed and changed the subject to how, after his first year of med school, he'd somehow gotten an audition for a touring company of *Rent*, even though he'd never been an actor and hadn't sung a lick since he was in the boys' choir. The casting director stopped him two bars in and called the next singer on but that one experience, he said, was a lot more fun than all the years he'd put in at med school.

"But I think I'm better off saving lives," he shrugged, "It's what I'm meant to do."

Nelson asked if I wanted *crème brûlée*. Nobody had ever asked me that before. In my head, I repeated the words, "*crème brûlée, crème brûlée*," as though I were rolling around in a whole vat of it.

Aloud, though, I said, "Lemme check my wallet."

As I went to reach for it, Nelson put his hand over mine, "I'll pay for it." I said, "Don't be silly." He said, "Come on. Please. How often do I get to take out a starving artist?" I wasn't sure if this was a rhetorical question but before I could hazard a guess, Nelson said, "Besides, you need to save your money. New York ain't cheap."

He was right. The last time I'd failed there proved that. I put my wallet away. The *crème brûlée* was delicious enough to put a muzzle on my ever-growling stomach.

Nelson offered to drive me home. We both wore bashful smiles as we walked the two blocks to his jet-black BMW. He opened my side first and closed it when I got in. Nelson hopped into the driver's seat and smiled as he turned the ignition.

"So, how do we get to your place?" he said as we headed east. I told him to take a few right turns and then there we were at my high rise, the waves breaking on the shore up ahead.

"Wait," he said, looking at the building, "You live here?"

I said, "Yeah."

He said, "But this is a nice place."

I didn't know what to tell him, so I went for a line, "Well, my other apartment is in the projects."

Nelson's face sunk.

After a few seconds of pro forma canoodling, I said good night and exited the BMW. My building's doorman let me in and I took the elevator nine floors up.

My phone didn't ring for the rest of the night. The next morning, I emailed Nelson to tell him I'd had a good time but he didn't write back. Despite myself, for the next several days, I'd call to check my answering machine but there were no messages from him. His online profile showed that he'd been active every day since our date and, by the next week, he had added pics of himself and his friends partying during the weekend he'd just spent in Baltimore.

It seemed when he'd written me, Nelson was in the market for a stray but instead had gotten a scruffy

AristoCat. It was time for him to call on the next character from *Rent*.

This was the last date I'd ever go on in Chicago. I decided to skip even more meals so I could move to New York even earlier. I traded in my $400-a-month apartment in a doorman building on the Chicago lakeshore for a studio in Fort Greene, Brooklyn that was half the size and two and a half times the rent.

Even that apartment was considered a steal, though, even after the broker's fee and two-month's deposit. Later I found out why I'd lucked into such a bargain. It was a backyard apartment that looked out on to an abandoned building where prides of feral cats lived. Now instead of falling asleep to the gentle undulations of waves, I was grinding my teeth to the sounds of female cats screaming bloody murder during mating season.

THICK & THIN

JULIUS: Kyle, I'd rather not lose friends over a disagreement. I'd rather lose them because they recognize themselves as characters in a novel that you sold for millions of dollars.

STEEPLECHASE

(*Julius comes back from his walk. He's been listening to an audiobook of* Anna Karenina.)

JULIUS: Well, *Anna Karenina* is really heating up. Anna just told Count Vronsky that she's in the family way and they're discussing options.

KYLE: Really? You know, I've made about 10 cracks at that book but I never reached that point. My eyes gave out.

JULIUS: Oh, it's a much different experience listening to it than reading it. Audiobooks are so much more immersive.—I'd hate to say that. It makes me sound like a rube.—But I tell you, when they were at the steeplechase, I was in Prospect Park and there were all sorts of horses out, you know, from the stables in Windsor Terrace. And I felt like I was there! In 19th Century Russia! I could literally smell the manure.

(*Beat*)

KYLE: (*Takes smartphone out of pocket*) Let me type what you just said while I still got you standing here.

VOCABULARY BUILDERS

I do have to admit to something and I'm not proud of it but this is the time to make this confession given what we have lurking in the White House.

When I was 10, I was the only kid in my class who didn't know what a pussy is. When I asked the other kids, they pointed and laughed and left me floundering in my ignorance.

So I went to my brother Kent and said, "Kent, what's a pussy?" He was 14 and he burst out laughing. "Why are you laughing at me?" I said, tears of shame rolling down my cheeks, "Everybody laughs at me. I just want to know what a pussy is!" This, of course, made him laugh harder and he was not about to inform me what a pussy is, given that two years before this moment, I'd gotten him grounded for two weeks for accidentally saying fuck when one of our shelving units collapsed. He let me swim in my tears.

Mom came in. "Kyle," she said, "What happened?"

I said, "Kent won't tell me what a pussy is."

Kent was on the floor at this point, laughing all the harder, which of course made me cry all the harder. Mom pled ignorance, "Well, isn't a pussy a cat?"

Now Kent was flushed and in a jiggling fetal position.

I wailed, "Even I know a pussy's not a cat, Mom! But what is it? Everyone else knows. And everybody's laughing at me."

Mom threw her hands in the air, "It's a cat. That's all I can tell you."

I ran out of the room.

Finally, I found another older brother. I said, "Please. Tell me. Just tell me. All the other kids at school know. I deserve to know too. What's a pussy?"

He sighed and leveled with me, "A pussy is a woman's vagina."

"Great," I said, wiping my eyes, "Now we're getting somewhere."

And breathing a sigh of relief, I added, "Now, what's a vagina?"

MT

(*Julius's cousin, who happens to be Jewish like Julius's father, has just passed the bar exam. Kyle sees this on Facebook.*)

KYLE: Oh my God! Daniel passed the bar!

(*Kyle starts typing his congratulations*)

JULIUS: Why are you typing "MT, dude!"

KYLE: Cuz it's the new *thang*! All the Jewish hipsters in Brooklyn are doing it! Don't you ever read Facebook?

JULIUS: MT?

KYLE: Um . . . *Mazel Tov*, anyone?

JULIUS: MT? Oh my God! What would my grandfather Abraham say?

KYLE: Well, imagine what my Grampa Barney would say.

THE FILIPINO NURSE

(Kyle and Julius towel off their eyes after "Terms of Endearment")

KYLE: I thought this was supposed to be a side-splitter.

JULIUS: No, Kyle. The caption said "tearjerker." Tearjerker. I don't know how you got "side-splitter" out of "tearjerker."

KYLE: Well I'm sorry. Not all of us are fancy lawyer types like you. We don't all spend our days looking at the fine print.

JULIUS: You do with the lines from your stories.

KYLE: Oh, speaking of lines…the mother's last lines to her son before Shirley MacClaine chases him down in the parking lot. I just…—What were your parents' last words to you?

JULIUS: I don't recall offhand. I wrote them down somewhere. I should look them up. What were yours to you, again?

KYLE: Well, my mother said, "I'm sure you'll be writing for *Downton Abbey* one of these days."

JULIUS: But it's off the air.

KYLE: Hey, nobody said she was a prophet.—And Dad died, what, 10 months later. All he said was, "Take care of yourself." He said it twice, in fact.

JULIUS: And he meant it too. He cut you out of the will.

KYLE: Yeah. Still, give him credit for not saying, "Take care of yourself…cos I sure as hell ain't gonna."—I guess I have a knack for remembering people's last words to me. You know, I was living with my Grampa all those years ago when he died.

JULIUS: Did he die at home?

KYLE: No. He was in the hospital.

JULIUS: And what were his last words?

KYLE: I don't know what his *last* last words were. But his last words to me were: "I hope you never have to experience the pain of a Filipino nurse twisting your testicles during a sponge bath." He pantomimed the experience with a wrenching fist. Then he collapsed back on to the bed and fell into a deep sleep. I stood there a few minutes and went home. He was gone a few days later. —You know, I wonder why he felt the need to mention that the nurse was Filipino. I mean, would it have been less painful if an Irish nurse had wrenched his nuts?

JULIUS: Maybe for him. People from his generation were far more apt to otherize.

KYLE: I suppose so. Although now that I think about it, I don't think I ever heard Grampa Ed use the word "otherize."

SOCIALISM

KYLE: Julius! (*Tugging the blankets back*) You do this every night!

JULIUS: What?

KYLE: You hog the blankets. By 3 am, I have chattering teeth and hypothermia.—From now on, we need an equal distribution.

(*Julius turns light on. Starts remaking bed.*)

JULIUS: My God! Even when you're half asleep you're a socialist.

SELF-PARENTING (LIKE A TOTAL DORK.)

There's a new barista at the place where I write. He's swathed in tattoos. He has two nose rings and cartilage piercings descending to his ear spools. His black hair is streaked with green, tasseled back and wrapped in a dark blue bandana. He is young-Axl-Rose-scrawny and wearing a Joy Division *Unknown Pleasures* t-shirt with the sleeves cut off.

He is at least 20 years younger than I am but all of a sudden I'm 14 again and thinking this guy is soooo *kewl*. But back when I was that age, a big part of being *kewl* was acting like you were sooo over-it. And I am. I'm 43. But now I'm back to being 14, so now I'm not over-it but I have to act like I am.

He says, "Hi."

A consummate adult in a J. Crew t-shirt and nothing punk about me anymore, I say, "Hi. Can I have an iced coffee and a Smart Water please?"

He reaches for the cups, "A large?"

"A large," I say riffling through my wallet like its ragged interior is so much more fascinating than the regression I'm undergoing.

As he digs the ice out of the icemaker, I say to my inner teenager, "No! You are not going to say you like his shirt and you are not going to say you saw Joy Division's last show in 1980. That's a flat-out lie. You were five in 1980. Plus the lead singer killed himself the day before they could even go on their U.S. tour. No fibbing. I forbid it."

My inner teenager calls me a dick, lights a Marlboro and wanders off somewhere. My 43-year-old self holds out payment like a battle-ax schoolmarm in a starched collar and pumps.

The barista puts the water bottle in front of me and says, "Do you think this Smart Water should apply for a MacArthur grant?"

"I'm sorry?" I say.

"You know what that is? A MacArthur grant?"

"Oh, you mean the Genius Award?"

"Yeah," he says with a Jeff Spicoli voice and Jeff Spicoli eyes, "The bottle should apply. I mean it is… *Smart*. Water."

So it's a dumb joke and he isn't giving me much to work with, but still he is trying to be friendly so I think I owe him a response. "Well," I say, "It is an inanimate object and it doesn't have a cerebral cortex so I don't know what its chances would be. But as long as it has an email account, it should at least download the forms. Of course, one doesn't *apply* for a Genius Award. The MacArthur Foundation *selects* its genius candidates. But who knows, maybe it's this bottle's lucky day."

He dead-stares at me. My inner teenager comes back and face-palms. I sidle away with my beverages and just like old times, I walk over to my table (in my J. Crew t-shirt, no less) feeling like a total dork.*

*Even though, arguably, he was a dork first with that MacArthur line.

PONTIUS PILATES

(The Monday after Easter)

JULIUS: Kyle, I have to tell you something. Something happened on Friday. Irena saw me do something and . . . it's better you hear it from me than from her.

KYLE: Irena, our cleaning lady? Okay, Julius, what's his name?—It wasn't the new ConEd meter-reader, was it? Oh, we've all swooned over him but some of us show restraint.

JULIUS: No. It was nothing like that. I . . . I went to Mass.

KYLE: You what!

JULIUS: Well, it was Good Friday. They had a Bach choral arrangement. I thought it'd be a good thing to do. I tried to sit toward the back and keep a low profile but Irena was there and she spotted me in the Communion line.

KYLE: Well. So much for making a clean break. Not exactly Henry VIII, now are we? Tell me, when did this whole affair begin?

JULIUS: Well, the Passion was at 3 p.m. You were working out downstairs.

KYLE: I thought there was something fishy about how you ordered the grilled branzino that night.

JULIUS: Well, I also thought it'd help immerse me in a course I'm taking on the Holy Roman Empire.

KYLE: You're taking a course on the Holy Roman Empire?

JULIUS: Yes, at Yale.

KYLE: At Yale?!?

JULIUS: But it's online.

KYLE: What else are you up to these days, may I ask?

JULIUS: Just boot camp and Pilates, I swear.

KYLE: You mean, Pontius Pilates? Boy, every time I turn my back . . .

THE PROFANATION OF ST. FRANCIS

My mother used to have a St. Francis fountain in what she called our *foyer*. It was a fancy French word she'd picked up somewhere or other, one that never failed to elicit a nod of approval whenever she'd introduce our *foyer* as such to whatever new members her church bridge club might recruit.

St. Francis had a sparrow perched on the forefinger of his upraised left hand. With his right hand, he held a seashell at his groin. What made the seashell's placement all the more unfortunate was that it was through the seashell that the fountain's water sprayed out. What made it more unfortunate still was that my mother had decided to redirect the flow of water through a floppy, flesh-colored rubber tube that she hung from the spigot in the seashell.

We told her what this looked like. She said she ought to scrub our minds out with soap. We told her we heard what the ladies in her bridge club were saying about it when she'd leave the room to get the coffee carafe. She said we were making up stories and that the ladies thought it was darling.

The next time she hosted bridge, though, the ladies didn't trickle in throughout the first half hour like they normally did. Instead they all came as a group, half an hour early—for an intervention.

They sat my mother down in the living room.

"Maureen," said Mrs. Moriarty, "We have to talk to you about that St. Francis fountain." Mrs. Moriarty bowed her head in preparation to deliver some home truths but when she looked up, she erupted into sniggers.

So did the rest of the ladies.

My mother asked if anyone wanted coffee and excused herself from the room.

Somewhere between pouring the coffee and setting out the milk and sugar, she turned off the fountain and yanked the flesh-colored tube out of the seashell that St. Francis held to his groin.

Water never flowed from it again.

SEI ITALIANO?

(*Locanda Vini e Oilii, Clinton Hill, Brooklyn*)

KYLE: What are you thinking about?

JULIUS: What makes you think I'm thinking about something?

KYLE: I know when you're thinking about something.

JULIUS: I was thinking about asking my bikram yoga teacher, "Sei Italiano?"

KYLE: You're thinking of asking him this because he's Italian?

JULIUS: Well, that—and because he's always singing opera to himself on the elevator.

KYLE: And they let him teach yoga class?

JULIUS: Oh, he's a phenomenal yoga instructor. But I get the sense that he's lonely.

KYLE: Could this have anything to do with how he sings opera on elevators?

JULIUS: Well, he's in great shape but he's single and I think there's something about him that pushes people away.

KYLE: I go back to my previous question.

An Audience of Teletubbies

Being a pretty weird guy, you can imagine I also have pretty weird dreams. So, last night, I was on the talk show of a green alien with silver antennae named Shinola who hosts a program called *Talking Shit with Shinola*. Shinola asked me who has been my greatest teacher. My answer was something I don't think I could've come up with in waking life but that I'm so glad was tucked away in my subconscious. I said, "My greatest teacher has been Osmosis."

Shinola said, "Oh, is Osmosis your girlfriend?"

I said, "Whoa, you don't know shit, do you Shinola? Osmosis is a process by which things just kind of slip in and your mind just kind of balances out. And if I just let myself relax into a state of attentive awareness, I always learn what I most need to know."

The studio audience, which was composed entirely of Teletubbies, gave me a standing ovation. This has never happened for me on earth, but apparently talk shows in outer space will have me on for a full hour.

SWINGERS

(*San Francisco—Kyle and Julius hit it off with the couple at the next table.*)

ISABELLE: So we should all hang out!

JOSH: Especially since you're new in town.

ISABELLE: And hey, you know, we're big swingers.

KYLE: Oh, well, we're not . . . into that.

JULIUS: I'm afraid we're a little old-fashioned.

ISABELLE: What's more old-fashioned than Count Basie and the Charleston?

JOSH: And you know, if it's a matter of not having the right suit, they sell them vintage up on Haight Street.

KYLE: Oh, those kind of swingers. I thought… *(To Julius)* Remember that time we met that couple from Westchester?

THE ALPACA GUY

(*Before show at MTC Theater, Julius is standing up at his seat, waving his arms off to someone.*)

USHER: (*approaches*) Yes, sir?

JULIUS: Oh, I wasn't waving at you.

USHER: Oh, okay.

(*Usher walks off. Julius continues standing, waving.*)

KYLE: Who are you waving at?

JULIUS: (*waving wildly*) Someone I used to work with.

KYLE: What's his name?

JULIUS: (*waving more*) I can't remember.

KYLE: What did he do there?

JULIUS: (*waving with abandon*) I'm not really sure.

(*Julius smiles, stops waving. Guy approaches.*)

GUY: Julius!

JULIUS: I thought that was you.

GUY: And you must be Kyle.

JULIUS: Yes, you've both heard a lot about each other.

(Kyle side-eyes Julius.)

GUY: Yep. I'm the guy with the Alpaca.

JULIUS: You own an Alpaca?

GUY: Well, yeah. What else would you have to tell him about me?

JULIUS: Well . . . what a good job you do at work.

THE ZAFU APOCALYPSE

That feeling when you're meditating and your text dings and you sit there afraid it's your husband texting to say that Ruth Bader Ginsburg died and you start having a panic attack on your meditation cushion, anticipating the end of the world, only to find out when the meditation timer rings that he was just texting to say he fed the cats.

MUDDER

(*Kyle walks past a contractor on 8th Av, Brooklyn.*)

CONTRACTOR: (*on cell phone*) So, he starts givin' me this cock-n'-balls story—

KYLE: (*interloping*) That's cock-and-bull story.

CONTRACTOR: D'ya mind? I'm tawkin' to my mudder.

JULIUS PREPARES THE JOINT TAX RETURN

JULIUS: On March 10th last year, you gave $150 to the GoFundMe site. What charity was that for?

KYLE: (*looks it up*) Oh, that was for Martin's friend.

JULIUS: Martin's friend, who?

KYLE: I don't know.

JULIUS: But you gave him a hundred and fifty dollars?

KYLE: He needed gall-bladder surgery.

JULIUS: Do you *know* him?

KYLE: Martin knows him. He sometimes speaks at his sangha.

JULIUS: Well, can you get a 501(c)(3) letter from the sangha?

KYLE: They don't have 501(c)(3) forms in England.

JULIUS: England!?!

KYLE: Yeah, England. Remember? We declared independence from them in 1776.

JULIUS: Kyle, charitable donations are not tax deductible in England.

KYLE: That's right. The English give out of the goodness of their hearts.

JULIUS: Oh, but I'll tell you what they *do* have in England, Kyle. They have the NHS. And they perform surgeries for free.

KYLE: Except the poor guy had to go out-of-network. It was an emergency situation, Julius. I can show you the post that Martin shared. It said the NHS would have waitlisted the guy a whole six months. He'd be dead by then.

JULIUS: Does the Prince of Nigeria make a cameo in this story?

KYLE: No. Martin posted it. He knows the guy personally. They're good friends. The guy runs soup kitchens in Newcastle. He teaches out-of-work coal miners how to meditate. The man is a saint. His wife posted a plea for donations and she was able to raise the funds within 24 hours.

JULIUS: Yeah, because you kicked in most of it.

KYLE: I did not. For however much $150 might seem, it was a drop in the bucket. People couldn't fill the kitty fast enough. I'm telling you, this guy was like the British George Bailey.

JULIUS: Except you don't know his name.

KYLE: Well I did, but I forgot it.

JULIUS: And can you get a letter from his wife?

KYLE: No. I gave anonymously.

JULIUS: Anonymously!

KYLE: Well, if you give for name rec, it's not true generosity, now is it? Anyway, my shrink was out of town that month. I had the money.

JULIUS: And how is this guy doing? Is he . . . "still with us"?

KYLE: Martin said he's back in action. The soup kitchen and sangha are up and operational again.

JULIUS: So I guess this was yet another deposit you made to our Karma Account.

KYLE: What, the universe didn't send you a statement?

JULIUS: It sure as hell isn't giving me a tax deduction.

NATURE

JULIUS: I like Sheldon. I do. But I think…I think he talks behind our backs.

KYLE: Of course he does. He's an old queen. Don't take it personal.

BREAKFASTS & NIGHTMARES

*June 25, 2016—Bloomsbury, London,
Two Days after Brexit Vote*

Last night, I had a nightmare that I walked into one of those 1960s British greasy spoons, like the ones you see in *Quadrophenia*. I ordered an English Breakfast. This was scary enough because I don't eat pork. Scarier still, the stout waitress walked over to my table with a cigarette dangling from her mouth and threw a plateful of English "Brexit" in front of me. It had a raw egg with a really raw deal on the side. I said I'd ordered an English Breakfast, not an English Brexit, but she said she couldn't take it back. I said, "I'm not paying for this," and walked out. I guess I was in Dover because I strolled over to the English Channel, where I was planning to walk on water over to France in search of better cuisine. Only before I could roll up my pant legs, all these walls started rising up, all around all the coasts. It was like the Berlin Wall was coming up all around the UK. There was no leaving.

I woke up with a start. Later, in waking life, Julius asked me if I wanted to have breakfast near the British Museum. I said, "No. Order breakfast around here and you might get a Brexit you can't send back."

DISTINCTION

KYLE: That's it! I'm throwing an I Ching on this one. I need three pennies. Is this your coin purse?

JULIUS: No. That is my coin *holder*.

Another Brexit Nightmare

*June 26, 2016—Bloomsbury, London,
Three Days after Brexit*

I had a dream last night that I'd developed a product called Brit Whip. It was Cool Whip, only with this kind of Cool Whip, every time you ate a scoop, you'd end up with a British accent. Best yet, if you ate enough of it, your British accent would last for days. The slogan was, "Brit Whip: Because Everything Sounds—And Tastes!—Better with a British Accent."

Well, Americans were literally and figuratively eating up my product. Stores were having trouble keeping Brit Whip in stock. There were massive back orders and trucks carrying Brit Whip had to park many blocks away from every grocery store in every city in America, lest they be mobbed by ravenous customers, and the deliverers would have to enter through each store's service entrance at undisclosed hours in the middle of the night.

Now, on the upside—Everyone in the United States, even in Oklahoma, who had started eating Brit Whip was walking around talking like the characters on

Downton Abbey. They were all employing such clever turns of phrases, you'd think most of the American public had been in finishing school taking elocution lessons from the Dowager Countess.

And all they had to do to acquire such refinement was eat!

Sure, since most people still weren't hitting the gym and they were eating what was essentially Cool Whip, they looked like hell.

But they were also becoming more sophisticated and Brit Whip consumers had even begun turning off their TVs and picking up books, thinking it would be so much fun to educate themselves and sound even more regal. Their ideas became more refined and a critical mass of Brit Whip eaters, otherwise known as the red-state electorate, began to gather together and discuss how a better, more enlightened world might be possible.

Now, as for me, I became the Jonas Salk of comfort-food manufacturers. True, I was becoming a rich man but I had been so gratified by the changes taking place in people's lives as they consumed Brit Whip that I decided to keep prices low and even developed Brit Whip Lite, a low-cal alternative to Brit Whip ("low in sugar, high in taste," as promised). Weight Watchers had even begun marketing it. Brit Whip Lite eaters now held the promise of not only sounding like but *looking like* Lady Mary.

Unfortunately, the rise in sales had coincided with the ever-rising popularity of Donald Trump's candidacy after he'd already won the Republican primary.

He was well-aware that there were bills in both British and Irish parliaments to ban him from entering the UK and the Republic of Ireland on account of his bigotry and hate speech.

By this time, Trump had accused me of warping the hearts and minds of good-hearted, God-fearing 'Muricans. In a flurry of monosyllabic tweets he said that I was trying to drag us back to the days when we were under the dominion of the Crown. Memes went viral with my face on Queen Elizabeth's profile with the title "The Queen." Trump told male voters that if they ate Brit Whip, they too would become queens. He even got the *Duck Dynasty* guys on board and they personally drove men to the polls in droves to vote for Trump on the promise that I'd be extradited for corrupting the bodies and minds of God-fearing just-plain-folks with my ever-affordable brand of Cool Whip.

To be clear, my own popularity hadn't diminished. But I was not running for public office. And rather than vote for Trump's opponent, my supporters—who were legion—had decided to honor me (or, *honour* me) by staying home and eating Brit Whip.

Trump had won in a landslide victory.

His first order of business: banning sales of Brit Whip.

His second: extraditing me.

I was fine, though. I have an Irish passport. I moved to Dublin.

But the Irish weren't interested in Brit Whip, as a rule.

I moved to London and tried marketing Brit Whip there but I kept hearing, "What's the point, mate? Already got th' accent."

I lost my whole fortune.

But a kind grocer in Brighton found me on the streets and gave me a job as a stock boy.

At night, I slept in his freezer, next to the Cool Whip.

BANG YER HEAD

JULIUS: *(To Kyle)* I had a dream about you last night. We were in a car elevator. You got out of the car, you got on your knees and you started banging your head against the wall. I screamed, "Kyle! What are you doing?"—And that's how I knew I was dreaming . . . because, in real life, I've learned not to ask.

ONE MONTH AFTER BREXIT

JULIUS: I don't think Brexit is going to go into effect. The government will figure out a way to step over the mess they made. I never found parliament to be too principled.

KYLE: Well, it's going to take a lot of gymnastics to turn this ship around.

JULIUS: Kyle, you can't turn a ship around by doing gymnastics.

KYLE: You can on the pommel horse. Ever see those guys? With their muscly arms? They turn themselves all around on that thing.

JULIUS: They're turning their bodies around on it, Kyle. They're not turning a ship around. They're on a pommel horse, not a ship. And they're not even turning the pommel horse around. It's stationary.

KYLE: Well, parliament can't turn this pommel horse around either.

JULIUS: You can never cop to a mixed metaphor, can you?

COLLUSION

As I was typing a message to my friend Victor in the Netherlands, autocorrect turned "horrible sociopath" into "hottie sycophant." Even my smartphone knows there are two sides to that coin.

OUDESCHANS:
AN EX-ALTAR BOY HASHES IT OUT WITH GOD ON THE EDGE OF THE RED LIGHT DISTRICT

"Welcome to Amsterdam! . . . Go fuck yourself."

These were the first words said to us after we got off the *fokker* at Amsterdam Airport Schiphol.

Little did we know that, come midnight, we'd be doing just what the man had told us to do.

The man was a car service driver holding up a sign to price-gouge any greenhorn who might want to bypass the taxi stand. Just like at JFK or LaGuardia, there were announcements all over the loudspeakers telling us not to accept rides from gypsy cab companies. So when the man said, "Welcome to Amsterdam!," presenting his company's sign with the flourish of a magician hatching a flapping dove from a silk scarf, Julius and I smiled and said, "No thank you," and that's when he told us to go fuck ourselves. This didn't faze us in the least. You hear much worse for much less in New York so we went on wheeling our luggage over to wait in line for the city taxis, as one is supposed to do.

That's one thing that Julius and I have in common. In just about every context of life, we hew closely to the rules for fear of penalties and danger. For Julius, it's because he's a securities lawyer. He's trained to think in terms of rules, regulations and procedures. For me, it's because Saturn is in Cancer in my natal horoscope.

In classical astrology, Saturn is the bearded, wizened tyrant who demands that we walk a narrow path and woe to those who don't. An astrologer friend said I have Saturn in the most difficult part of my chart—the fourth house of family, home and upbringing. It's why I was born into an authoritarian Catholic household with a former Marine corporal father, who liked to call himself *The Great Santini* and rule by the belt, instead of into the progressive family I'd always longed for where Mom comes in with a tray full of French toast, mimosas and mint-flavored condoms for you and your boyfriend when you wake up in the same bed the morning after prom. My Saturn placement is apparently where I got my early and extreme fear that allowing myself the slightest license will seal my doom forever. It's the thing I like least about myself.

It's also the thing I like least in other people, which is why I lobbied so hard for this vacation in Amsterdam. It was April 2016 and the American airwaves were filled with all the latest invectives hurled from Republican primary-campaign podiums. Trump was demolishing his opponents with schoolyard taunts and shoring up his base with Nazi-style rallies that made WrestleMania look like a Mensa convention. He promised to build a wall and round up the undocumented and, by the end of the year, he would even promise to institute a Muslim registry—something the Anne Frank House alone will show you is way up there on the list of the cruelest things a government can do. Meanwhile Trump's opponents on the right were ratcheting up their hyper-churchy, anti-gay and anti-immigrant rhetoric, hoping their bigotry would trump his, but no matter how hard they tried (and Good Lord, how they tried!), Trump's bigotry had theirs licked.

If I were going to have any peace during my time off that year, I would have to go someplace tolerant, enlightened, and far away from home. I'd been to Europe countless times but had never made an effort to go to Amsterdam. It had a reputation for being one big fleshpot and, what with Saturn's stranglehold over my every impulse, I had to face that I'm just not that much of a hedonist. Yet more and more I'd also been hearing about and reading up on how Amsterdam isn't the junkie juggernaut that so many people make it out to be.

The Dutch are simply practical in ways that would make Middle American puritans clutch their pearls and stockpile their front-hall closets with assault rifles. Point all the guns you want at people, they're still going to visit prostitutes. You might as well legalize it, regulate it, tax it and generate revenue from it for improved infrastructure and the common good. People are going to do soft drugs so you might as well legalize them, regulate them, tax them and generate revenue from them so people are less inclined to hit the harder stuff on the black market. Teenagers are going to have sex so you might as well give them comprehensive sex ed and teach them how to protect themselves from pregnancy and disease. Illnesses can reach such advanced and incurable stages that, if we were to see our beloved animal companions in the throes of them, we'd say it's cruel to keep them going—so why insist that people experience every torturous moment of a terminal illness with only the aid of opioids? Why not offer them the option, if they're still of sound mind, of having a peaceful and medically induced end if they so choose? As a result of all these practical reforms, sex workers are licensed and protected from pimps, the government is far better able to detect and crack down on human trafficking, people can die with dignity and there is far less drug abuse and far lower teen pregnancy rates per capita in the Netherlands than in the United States.

My Dutch friend Victor and I discuss this subject *ad nauseum* over email. A few months before our trip, I happened to make friends with Victor on a meditation app called Insight Timer. After a period of discussing our meditation practices with each other on the app, we soon began to write each other long and winding emails in which we'd compare and contrast our cultures. I'd bemoan the Christian right and he'd remind me that I live in New York City, I have sanctuary. He'd tell me that the Netherlands has a Bible belt too and that Geert Wilder's far-right party is constantly stoking hatred of Muslims. At the same time, while it's true that

Amsterdam has long prided itself on its openness and tolerance, it is almost impossible to be openly gay in some of its more conservative Muslim communities. He said I'd have to live there to know that, for all its upsides, Holland is not a failsafe safe-space for liberalism nor is it a holiday from the dark side of human nature.

Julius and I made plans to meet Victor in person on the second day of our trip but we still had this first day to get through, and it's our first day that is the subject of this essay.

Far from being one of the Cities of the Plain, I found that Amsterdam is a city of adorable sloping metal bridges lined with old-fashioned gas lamps. It's a city of tree-lined, cobblestone streets, where men are not ashamed to ride bicycles with wicker baskets and bells on their handlebars. Prismatic tulip gardens bloom in profusion in Amsterdam's parks and on its parkways. Boats sail through rings of canals, built in the seventeenth-century, while other boats sit docked on the side, uncovered and unmolested even in a city of nearly one million people. Young people drink their lagers with leisure at the outdoor cafes instead of slyly looking around and pounding them back before they can get caught, since what's the point of doing that when they've already reached the drinking age?

Julius and I were staying in an Airbnb on the second floor of a slim, four-story townhouse with a gabled roof on Oudeschans, right across the canal from the red-light district. That's another practicality the Dutch have down. When it was first starting out as a major city,

Amsterdam's architects knew to design narrow houses since, in those days, property taxes were based on the building's width.

We rented an efficiency apartment made of plain wooden floors, plain wooden walls and a white-wooden lean-to. A plain wooden wardrobe stood next to our queen-sized Ikea bed, which was covered in a dove-white duvet. A plain wooden desk with a plain wooden chair stood across from the foot of the bed, where I could do my writing every morning. The landlord had placed a No Smoking sign on top of the full-length black TV by the black-bricked fireplace. We had what we needed in the apartment, plain and simple.

Julius would be pulling out all the stops for dinner, though. He'd booked us a table for two at Ciel Bleu, a two-star Michelin restaurant clear across town on the 23rd Floor of the Okura Hotel. It was an alarming contrast to the coffeshops we passed, where the denizens we spied through the windows sat at grungy tables letting their hair fall in their faces as they pulled long drags off roaring reefers, as well as to a certain red-lit vestibule we passed in the red-light district where a raven-haired woman in an open blouse stood in the window rolling her breasts in opposite directions with the speed of a batter-mixer on full blast. Our table by the window at Ciel Bleu had panoramic views of the city and, more close-up, of blocks and blocks of courtyard apartment buildings from the 1920s and '30s that were built in the expressionist style of The Amsterdam School, a movement that provided housing for working-class families in buildings whose facades are decorated with stained-glass windows, wrought ironwork and ornamental masonry lush with cornices and medallions.

There were several courses to this dinner that included Japanese Wagyu, Langoustine drenched in combava (which I later learned is froufrou for lime) and Baeri caviar. Though there were wine pairings galore, we still managed to wash it all down with a bottle of Bollinger champagne. Civilized and fabulous though the dining experience was, I couldn't help but think that Ciel Bleu isn't where the action is in Amsterdam. It's impossible to pull off an edgy act in such a five-star setting so instead I went full Dimitri Karamazov when I leaned in to *psst*-whisper, "We should smoke weed tonight." Julius took a sip of Bollinger and said, "We don't smoke weed. We smoke *hash*."

A year or so before we met, Julius had gone to Marrakesh where he'd smoked hashish for the first time. It was something he had arranged through the hotel's concierge. A male attendant, wearing a traditional white *djellaba*, had accompanied Julius to a roomful of ornately stitched throw pillows, where he prepared and lit a pipe that Julius held to his lips for several hits. The attendant, who had stayed sober and alert throughout the time that Julius smoked, promptly accompanied Julius back to his hotel room and turned out all the lights once Julius was tucked away in bed. It was all very Sebastian Flyte in *Brideshead Revisited*. Under the spell of the hashish, Julius hallucinated that he was floating through space inside a genie bottle full of throw pillows and shirtless, beefcake sultans in red turbans. All in all, he remembered it as a most relaxing experience.

We stayed for dessert at Ciel Bleu, ordering the chocolate tray, but I didn't pick from it much since I wanted to get a move on to the coffeeshops. Saturn was seizing up on me hard, of course, but I told myself I'd lived too long under his yoke. Sure, I'd tried pot a few times in college but it made me feel sleepy and depressed every time, not to mention that, as a former altar boy, the times I'd done it had filled me with the terror that I'd walked through the doorway into a no-tell motel of decadence and devastation from whence there was no return. There was a whole world of people out there, though, who weren't so uptight about these things and I wanted to be one of them. Now was the time to declare my freedom from Saturn, Amsterdam-style.

By the time we settled the bill at Ciel Bleu, we'd Googled "Best Coffeeshops for Hashish in Amsterdam." *TimeOut* recommended Greenhouse, which is next door to the Grand Hotel. It said Greenhouse had won the prestigious Cannabis Cup over 30 times. Julius said, with that kind of reputation, "It must sell a well-regulated product." I told him that many people had warned me that this is not the kind of no-additives marijuana that used to go around in the sixties and seventies. In Amsterdam, they jack up the THC (tetrahydrocannabinol), the mind-altering agent in both hashish and marijuana. I'd been warned that one joint would be the equivalent of ten. Julius said, "We'll be fine." I set the GPS on my phone for Greenhouse and we decamped to suck the marrow out of the Dutch capital.

Revelers swarmed the streets as we stalked the river Amstel via the Rokin into De Wallen. By turns, after giving take-a-left, take-a-right kinds of directions in standard American English, Garmin's voice would suddenly go dead-ringer Swedish Chef as she dished up Dutch street names like *De Gelderskade, Zeedijk* and *Enge Kerksteeg*. It was only about 10 p.m. at this point but some British guys in their late teens or early twenties were already yelling at a friend who was puking up his guts against the window of a bakery that had closed for the day: *"Come on, matey. We got a whole night still to get through."* We averted our eyes and plugged up our noses as the guys fought over who was going to look after their self-befouled friend. Meanwhile some American college girls were hyena-shrieking and yowling as they fell drunk and stoned to their knees while holding on to each other on the sidewalk, their frat-brother friends stepping in to pull them back up but having no luck since they were just as bombed as the college girls. Julius and I did what we always do when we encounter our fellow countrymen abroad—sped up and moved along.

At this point, the universe stepped in: My GPS died. My phone still had plenty of battery and all my other apps still worked, but somehow the GPS had given out. I pressed and pressed the icon but there was no reviving it. At the same time, Julius's phone had run out of battery so we were completely reliant on my phone for directions.

Now, here's where I have to confess something: one of the things that I've never been able to shake from my

Catholic past is my belief in a Higher Power. Never, never once, have I ever tried to get anybody else to believe in God, and many, many times I've been jealous of those who don't. For a long time, I tried being an atheist. It must be lovely to think you're not being watched all the time or that your every action isn't being accounted for on a karmic ledger. But I just couldn't believe these things deep down. Whether it was my parents' religious zealotry or 12 years of Catholic education, capped off by Jesuits, or whether there's just a part of me that somehow "knows," I've just always believed in what many call God.—To be clear, I've never bought into the idea that Jesus was/is God. I don't believe that the Bible is the word of anybody but the guys who wrote it, the guys who made God into their own highly biased and often bigoted and chauvinistic image. But I do have this unshakeable belief in God and his helpers, sometimes called angels, in ways I've never been able to explain and in ways I could never justify to a rationalist, which is why I tend to keep my mouth shut on the subject.

Yet I feel the need to mention it here because, when my GPS went out, I regarded it as a sign. A sign saying, "Turn back. *Now!*" Nonetheless, I persisted. I wasn't going to let my inner worrywart win this time. Not when I'd come this far. "We're going," I said to Julius. "How?" he said, "We don't know the way." I turned around and saw that, up the street, there was a place with bongs and pipes on display in the window. "There's a head shop right there," I said, "Let's ask."

We walked in and behind the counter sat a scraggly young man, who couldn't have been more than 20, though his face was already developing much the same road map of lines, scores and scabs as Keith Richards. He had a bleached Eminem Caesar cut and was rolling a fat joint in his spider-web-tattooed hands. "Hi," we said. In a Swedish-Chef-meets-2Pac voice, he said, "I'm all out, man. I'm all *out*," he made a cutting gesture with the inked-out fingers of his right hand as he gave us the kind of killer eyes that MMA fighters give each other right as they're about to square up. I brushed it aside and said, "Where's Greenhouse?" He huffed and shook his head, "Vot the fuck, man? Cross the bridge." We thanked him and he went back to rolling his joint with a dismissive *pfft*.

Prince Charming was right, though. Across the bridge stood the great and wondrous Greenhouse, shining like the Emerald City, albeit in lurid awning lights for the benefit of those who had already completed their tour and would probably find even moonlight too hard on the eyes. As we entered, we saw pretty much what we'd expected to see—dreadlocked white American Trustafarians in retro 90s grunge gear droning in strained, nasally voices over their European counterparts who were slung out and toking with Serge Gainsbourg savoir-faire on the low-slung leather couches. The walls were plastered with autographed photos of American celebrities who'd gone in to exercise their freedom—Snoop Dogg, Bill Maher, Eminem.

I steeled myself as Julius inspected the menu board above the counter. I let him decide what we'd be smoking since he tends to know what's best for us when it comes to real-world matters. (Having said that, if you're looking for line-edits on your cover letters, I'm your guy.) After sussing out every item on the board, he ordered us two of Greenhouse's Hash Joints, which consist of high-grade marijuana mixed with King Hassan Polm, a highly concentrated hash named after a 19th Century Moroccan monarch. As he rolled our joints behind the counter, the Kirk Hammett doppelganger in the Soulfly t-shirt said, "This is strong stuff, man." He locked eyes with Julius to underscore his point. Julius met him with a long and knowing nod as he stood boldly in his blue North Face Gore-Tex coat, which he'd made sure to pack since there was rain in the forecast for tonight and the rest of the week. The barista put each joint into a plastic tube and handed them over. Julius asked if we could smoke them outside. The guy said, "Yeah, just watch out for cops." We thanked him and paid at the register.

There were a couple stools available, right next to each other, at one of the smoking counters but Julius said, "Let's go home." I said, "No, let's smoke with the people." There was a lot of back-and-forth on this one but I ultimately prevailed. First of all, the No Smoking sign in the apartment was plain as day. Secondly, though I was no authority on Dutch law, I deduced that it probably wouldn't be legal for us to step out to the canal outside the apartment to smoke if we were already being warned to watch out for cops on the sidewalk right outside Greenhouse. I grew up in Chicago where cops come out of the woodwork. I wasn't going to see myself go up the river for getting stoned on a foreign canal. Julius said, "I think this is a mistake." I said, "Oh… come on!" in a quit-being-such-a-snob tone.

We took the joints out of the tubes and leaned against the counter stools. Julius lit mine and then his. I took a deep, deep diaphragmatic drag. As a longtime meditator and dharma student, who used to take classes in Kundalini yoga, I know how to breathe deeply and attentively. I had also been a cigarette smoker from ages 14 to 23, the age at which I decided to quit cold-turkey in an effort to bring into conscious awareness the reason why I was indulging such a bad habit. (The reason turned out to be a bit anticlimactic. Basically, after a lifetime of being talked down to, I wanted to be looked up to, so I did something I thought looked cool and sophisticated. Still, once I admitted to myself that was the reason, I never smoked a cigarette again.) I knew how to take deep drags and let out long, languid streams of smoke without choking or coughing.

Whatever this shit was that I was smoking, though, it tore through me like a California wildfire. And yet, even after two hits, I felt nothing. No numbness, no prickling sensations, not even a little lightheadedness. I took a third drag, and same deal. Maybe I was one of those rare people you hear of who's just not effected by these things, kind of like a Tibetan lama I'd once read about who surprised his student by swallowing all of the student's LSD in one gulp without feeling any side effects because his eons of meditation training had rendered him superhuman. In any case, I didn't enjoy the joint.

Just as I thought: it wasn't my thing. I stubbed it out and turned to Julius, all ho-hum and ready to leave.

Julius was going to town on his joint, though. He was taking hit after hit. So I did what I do when he's taking too long inspecting every item at Bed, Bath and Beyond. I tapped my foot, looked around, fumbled with my smartphone and looked around some more. Julius kept right on smoking.

Until at last, he cashed his joint out in an ashtray and put the half-burnt butt back into the plastic tube. "Ready?" he said with happy-camper eyebrows. I nodded.

As we made our way to the door, however, he began to shake. No longer ambling, he was now *tottering* across the threshold. If he'd held his arms out in front of himself, he'd have been Mary Shelley's monster. "You're going to have to lead the way," Julius said in a quavering voice, "I'm feeling a total loss of control."

No sooner had he said this than my own hash trip kicked in. The sidewalk in front of Greenhouse started to lap through waves of air like a flying carpet or like the genie bottle that Julius had thought he was bobbing through outer space in on his Moroccan hash trip. I knew this wasn't a good thing. There was no attendant, sent by the concierge, to get us back to our room and tuck us snugly under the covers and, it turns out, I wasn't the invincible Tibetan lama after all. Nonetheless it was up to me to get us out of this jam. Julius, the most capable person I know, had already declared himself incapable. I immediately started praying in silence, "Alright, God, I know I did this. I know I shouldn't have. But see, the thing is . . ."

"I'm starting to panic," Julius announced, "I'm *panicking.*"

I said, "Well, don't p*aaaaaa*nic…," and right as I said this, I noticed that I was speaking in the same pinched, wasteland voice as one of the junkies who held Jesse Pinkman up in that one *Breaking Bad* episode—I'm talking about the one where the meth-head pushed the stolen ATM on to her guttersnipe boyfriend's head when he was on the ground trying to unscrew the machine's bottom hatch to get the money out, and all because he called her a "skank." ("I'm not a sk*aaaaa*nk," she brayed over the smooshing of brains and the snapping and crackling of skull bones.)

Julius also happened to have watched that episode and he also happened to notice some resonance between her voice and mine. Now he was shrieking as people, including Grand Hotel guests, passed by. To calm him, I went up and held him. I was trying to duplicate the experience of a nanny holding a scared child but the effect was more that of Nancy Spungen cradling Sid Vicious as he's going cold turkey on the graffiti-swashed subway in *Sid & Nancy.*

Julius pulled himself together as much as he could manage and shrugged me off. "We gotta get outta here," he told me with a calm but sharp edge. "If we don't, I'm going to freak out. I'm just going to *freak out.*"

Silently, I prayed, "God, please help us," as Oudezijds Voorburgwal and all the people on it went in and out of focus and the street flapped like one big flying carpet in the wind. I took my smartphone out of my pocket. It felt light as air. I pressed the button to pull up the password screen but my tactile senses were so off, my thumb didn't seem to be making any contact with the numbers no matter how hard I pressed down. It took a good eight or nine tries but finally the screen sprang up. Luckily, I remembered my password. Yet as I typed it in, I felt as though my fingers were poking through all the way to the rubber back cover. Julius said, "I'll hold it! I'll hold it, okay? I'll hold it...and you, you *presssss*." It must have been Divine Intervention because I don't think I typed in all four of the numbers in my password. The high was so overwhelming, it seemed completely beyond my capacities to key them all in. Yet just as I was about to shove off in a doorway and curl up for a hard cry, all my apps sprang up.

Julius ruffled, "What's our address?"

I said, "Eeeeee…You, you don't, don't know *eet*?"

He said, "No, I don't know *eet*."

I said, "Well I don't know *eet* either."

He darted his head this way, that way and the other way, "Does anybody else here know *eet*?"

I screwed up my eyes, "How could they know *eet*? We're the only ones who know *eet*." Suddenly I remembered—"Wait, wait. I sent it to Victor. I sent it to Victor on WhatsApp." I started laughing, "Oh my God! Victor is coming over tomorrow and I totally fucking sent it to him! I sent Victor our address on WhatsApp. Holy fuck! I fucking…"

"Well pull up WhatsApp" Julius commanded.

There began another drill of steadying the phone between our persons as we each took turns trying to exert enough pressure to open the app without falling through the phone. And then it was a whole other battle opening up the messages between Victor and me, but somehow we managed again. I knew I couldn't call Victor, though. I couldn't have him meet me for the first time when I was like this. I said, "Okay, okay, okay. We're staying at 1— Oudeschans. Remember that. 1— Oudeschans. Or…I'll remember 1—, and you remember Oudeschans. Okay? Got it? Got it? Okay. Now let's get a cab."

I started walking through a thick nighttime crowd that faded in and out of focus as Julius held the back of my black raincoat, saying, "There's no such thing as cabs here! This isn't New York."

Yet I screamed, "Taxi!" and a taxi pulled up alongside me as I reached the curb.

"Alright alright alright," Julius said, "Just, just…get in."

We piled into the cab and I said, "*Hiiiii*," to the cab driver as though he was the concierge-sent attendant we'd been waiting for all along.

"Hello," said the driver.

"Could you take us to," I said, putting my hand in the front pocket of the dress pants that I'd worn to Ciel Bleu. Yet as I slid my hand down the pocket, I felt no smartphone. "Shiiiiiit!!!!! Julius!!! I dropped my phone out there on, on, on…Oh shit, on…"

"What?" Julius screamed from the seat next to me, shaking, "What did you do?"

"I dropped my fucking phone out, out there on… on the…"

"Oh shit!" Julius raged, "On the sidewalk! Fuck, we…We'll never find it. Somebody else has it. They'll rob you as soon as look at you in this drug den of a city. Let's, let's get back out. We, we have to find it. We have to find it. There's no not-finding-it. We're dead if we don't find it. But we'll never find it."

"I'm so sorry, sir," I said to the driver.

"It's okay," he said as we rushed out of the cab to comb each concrete slab on Oudezijds Voorburgwal but just as I was about to slam the taxi door behind me, I put my hand inside the left pocket of my raincoat and there it was. *The phone!* "Julius!" I cheered, "I have it! I have it! I've got the phone! I've got the phone!" He looked at me incredulously but I held the phone aloft like Excalibur. He came darting toward me and, swinging the cab door back open, we clambered back into the back seat.

"Okay, sir," I said, "Sorry about that. So so sorry about that. Just take us to. Wait? Where's he taking us?"

Julius staggered, "I don't know."

"But you were supposed to remember the name of the street."

"No, I was supposed to remember the number," he said, "You were supposed to remember the *name* of the street."

"No, no. That's not how it worked at all. I was supposed to remember the—the…What was I supposed to remember again?"

It was at this point that I noticed that the cab hadn't moved since we'd gotten in. We were still idling on the curb in busy traffic. I reassembled. "Hold on, sir. This is going to take a second. You see, I have to press my password and then I have to go to WhatsApp and then after that, I have to get the address from…What's my friend's name, again?"

The cab driver must have been sent from heaven because any other cabbie in the world would have killed us by now, or at least ordered us to get out, but this guy actually said, "Take your time," even as cars were laying on their horns, which I've heard it takes a lot to get the Dutch to do.

The driver's calm somehow pacified me to the point where I could effectively punch in all the necessary keys, apps and messages to find the address. Yet now, as I tried to read the screen, the letters and numbers were swimming all about each other like alphabet soup or a school of seals. "Sir," I said with bated breath, "Could you just read this please? Read this, please. And take us there."

I held the smartphone over the divider but lost my dexterity and it fell out of my hand and bounced off the seat, hitting the front floor and sliding over to the heel of the driver's shoe.

"Oh this is just fucking *stelllll-ar*!" Julius rumbled.

I watched my smartphone hit the floor with the same awe and paralysis that one might watch their wedding ring go down an open drain in a public-restroom sink.

Yet, miraculously, when the cabbie reached down and picked the phone up, the screen had not switched off. It stayed the way it was. "Oudeschans," he read aloud,

"Okay. I know. I know. I take you," and he handed me back my smartphone.

"Thank you, sir," I said with the same plaintive tone that one would have toward the SWAT team member who picked off the home-invader who was holding them at gunpoint. I collapsed back into my seat, ready to be shuttled home with the kind of *deus ex machina* that the U.S. diplomats had toward the end of *Argo*.

"Where are you from?" asked the cab driver.

I smiled, "New York."

"Oh, New York," said the driver, "'Swonderful city."

Julius whispered to me, "I don't trust him."

"Why?" I whispered back.

"He knows what's going on," said Julius, "He knows the shape we're in. He's going to drive us to his gang of thugs and they're going to steal our wallets and…"

"Would you relax?" I said with all the tact of a Chinese star, "It's a city cab. See? It even has a meter."

"How…how does he know where we're going?"

"We'll be home soon," I said, taking a deep breath—of air, this time.

Four or five more blocks into the ride, Julius started hyperventilating and, at a stoplight, he unbuckled his seatbelt and scrambled out of the car, gasping for breath. "I have to get out of this car. I have to get out of this car," were the contrail of words he left in his wake.

He ran up to a stone bench at a cul-de-sac. I didn't even look at the final total on the meter. I just took my wallet out and threw a bunch of Euros at the driver. "Sorry, sir," I said, running out to look after Julius. In my haste, I must have given the driver a sizable tip because, instead of shouting that I owed him more, he shouted, "Oh, thank you, sir! Thank you!" and sped off.

I sat with Julius on the stone bench. Just as Alice's voice would change when she'd try reciting poems when talking to the Caterpillar and other underworld freaks, my larynx had gone all froglike as I said, "Do you, ergh, have to go to, ergh, the hospital?"

"NO," Julius said, "I just need to sit for five minutes."

I circled the stone bench in a daze, at times making airplane wings with my arms. People stared a bit, but not too much. I'm sure they'd seen worse in these parts. I paused again, folded my hands and gazed up into the stars, "God, help us."

No sooner had I said this than Julius shouted out, "Oudeschans."

I turned around. "What, ergh?"

"*Oudeschans.* I remember now. *Oudeschans. Oudeschans.* Now I remember it. I remember it and I won't forget it. Oudeschans."

By now, he'd repeated it so much I couldn't forget it either, no matter how stoned I was. "But how, ergh, do, ergh, we get, ergh, there?" I said, a whole lily pad full of frogs in my throat.

Julius breathed heavy, "I don't know. I don't know I don't know I don't know idontknow idontknow. We'll, we'll have to find some place. We'll have some place we can trust. And then, and then, we'll have to find *someone* in that place we can trust."

"How do we do that?"

"I don't know!" Julius exploded, pulling his hair.

"Alright alright alright," I said, turning him around toward what looked to be a pretty central part of town.

We walked on. It wasn't easy. My feet felt like they weren't making contact with my socks, much less with the ground. Yet I was still the steadier of the two of us. Figures blurred before us both but at least I knew to step out of their way. Julius was on the verge of walking straight into them. I shepherded him an inch or two to the left or right of each passerby but he elbowed me off.

"Stop holding me like I'm your, your, your *ward*," he said through gritted teeth, "You have to look tough around here."

I said, "How're you gonna do that in a Gore-Tex coat, Julius? And besides, you're running into people. I mean, actually running into them."

"I know *exactly* what I'm doing," he said, recovering his first tone of confidence since we left Ciel Bleu.

This was hopeful.

What was even more hopeful was that just up ahead, there was an Irish pub called McDonaugh's or Kitty O'Shea's or Mrs. O'Leary's Cow or Darby O'Gill or… the point is the Shamrock on the sign was unmistakable. This was an Irish pub.

"Your people," Julius stood in homage to the sign.

"Can they, ergh, get us home?" I said like Julius was The Scarecrow, The Lion and The Tin Man all rolled up into one.

"It's worth a shot."

We bungled in.

"Can. Ergh. You. Ergh. Help. Ergh. Us?" I said.

The snowy-haired man said in a brogue, "Have ya been smokin'?" miming the roach of a joint pinching his lips.

"*Yesssss*," I said with the desperation of the last suspect of a murder mystery. "But I assure you, sir…I've never done this before…"

A line of late middle-aged Brits, most of them women, sat at the bar and looked at me piteously. "Awww," they said in unison. One said, "Come over here, darling," and she and her husband made space for me next to their chairs at the end of the bar. I stood next to her husband, "I've never done this before!," I cried with something approaching the pathos with which The Elephant Man proclaimed, "I Am Not An Animal!" This elicited another big "Awww…"

"Did somebody put something in my joint?" I pled with the bartender.

He and everyone listening said in chorus, "Nooooo…"

"You'll be right as rain in a few hours' time," said the august Irishman. That is, before he turned to Julius and said, "Your friend here, he doesn't look well, mate. He's paler than a ghost." You know you're in bad shape when your paleness stuns an Irishman. I put my hands on the bar and tried to make small talk with the Brits. I recall that they said they were from Devon and liked to holiday in Amsterdam and I recall that, as I leaned on my hands, I felt as though I was falling through the bar.

By now, Julius was somehow able to shake off his high and talk and act normally, "Is there something you can give him?"

"I have just the thing," said the Irishman, "It's a milk and honey concoction with a wee bit of whiskey. Is your mouth dry, son?"

"Oh, ergh, yes, ergh," I said.

"We have just the thing for you," said the Irishman as he began to make the drink.

"Perfect," said Julius, "Thank you. Say, do you know a street called Oudeschans?"

"Oh, yes," said the man as he took the milk out of the mini-fridge below the bar, "Two streets that way and across the bridge. You can't miss it."

"Thank you," said Julius, "Can I use your bathroom?"

"Yes," said the Irishman, "Down the stairs and to the left."

"No, Julius," I said, "Don't go down the stairs. You'll fall. I mean, look at me. I'm *falling* through the bar." One of the English guardian angels brought me a stool and I sat down on it. "Thank you, thank you," I said as if these guardian angels were a fire brigade that just got my cats out of a tree.

"Can you look up the address while I'm down there, Kyle?" said Julius.

I pulled out my smartphone. By now, I'd regained enough manual dexterity to pass through my phone's password portal. I could even get to the message I sent to Victor with my address in it. What I still couldn't do, however, is *read* the damn thing. I squinted at the Englishman, "Excuuse, ergh, me, ergh, sir-ergh. I'd, ergh, hate, ergh, to, ergh, trouble, ergh, you. But, ergh, could you, ergh, write, ergh, this, ergh, down?" I pointed to the address.

"No worries, mate," said the Englishman, "Oi, Aloysius! Have you got a pen?"

The Irishman came by with a pen and a slip of paper.

"Aloysius?" I said, "That, ergh, was, ergh, my brother's, ergh, confirmation name, ergh. Can you, ergh, believe he was the only, ergh, one who, ergh, who chose it?"

"I'm not surprised," said the Englishman.

The Irishman brought over my convalescent milk and honey drink, "Ah, you're a Catholic lad then?"

"Well, not me, ergh," I said. "But my family, ergh. And we're, ergh, Irish."

"Oh I knew there was something I liked about ya," said the Irishman. "And your friend there? Is he an Irish lad?"

"Friend?" I said. "You mean, my, ergh, husband?"

"Oh, husband," said the Irishman nodding as he pulled a pint of Guinness that another customer had ordered.

"Yeah," I said, "They have, ergh, homosexuals, ergh, in Ireland too." I don't know why I said this but I did.

"Oh I do know that, laddy," said the bartender, nodding, "Some of my own seed and breed are of the kind. It's grand."

"But, ergh, where is he, ergh?" I said, looking every which way for Julius.

"I'm right here," said a voice. I turned to look and Julius was right next to me.

"Here you go, mate," said the Englishman, handing me back my phone and the piece of paper he'd written the address on.

I pocketed my phone and handed Julius the address. With a bleary stare, I ribbitted, "You, ergh, are, ergh, a kind, ergh, man."

"Am I?" he said, taking a swig of his drink.

His wife patted his back.

I nursed my milk, honey and whiskey nectar.

Somehow having recovered himself, Julius thanked the Irishman profusely and gave him a whole 20 Euros for the drink.

"Your partner's coming to," said the Irishman. "He'll be grand soon."

I finished my drink and the Irishman and the man from Devon walked us out and showed us the way home. I hugged them both. Julius just shook hands. They went back in.

It started raining.

After letting him off easy in the bar, Julius's hash kicked in again on the street, "Where did he say Oudeschans was again?" He looked every which way for the men but they were gone and we had ventured on to a street that neither one of us recognized.

Before I could panic all over again, I plucked up my wits and took out my phone. I punched in the password and clicked on the maps icon. Suddenly it worked! I handed the phone over to Julius so he could type in the address.

"To 1— Oudeschans," said Garmin.

My GPS was working again.

We huddled together as midnight approached and rain fell. We followed the map on the screen. Now Garmin was going full Rose Nylund, saying names that sounded like *Gerflingaflugin* and *Johannabugin.*

"How do we know we can trust her?" said Julius in reference to the phone.

"Don't start that again," I said.

"But I don't know if I can trust her." He began shuddering.

"It says on the screen it's only a block away."

"But...but...this is Europe," said Julius, "There could be satellite problems. And it's raining. We might have to spend the night on the streets."

"It's only a block away, it says."

"But how can we trust her?" said Julius.

"Julius, Garmin doesn't have plans to lead us down a back alley and mug us."

Truth be told, I didn't know this for sure either. All I knew was Garmin was all we had now. Yet, as we crossed the bridge over the canal, I could not place the address that we were nearing from the row of buildings. My breath caught. I said another silent prayer for help.

All of a sudden, Julius said, "Oh, there it is. There it is. We're here."

And there it was. Our building, rising from the mist of rain like Camelot, or so it seemed to me after the night we'd had.

We crossed the street to our building and weren't even run down by a big-wheeled bicycle.

My depth perception was a bit off as I tried to work the key in the front lock, though. After a few attempts, I managed the key but my hand felt so funny on the knob, I couldn't push the door open, so Julius held the door steady as I turned the key with as much precision as I could muster. Once I had it all the way to the right, Julius let go of the door and we both fell into the vestibule. We were home. We were safe.

But then I balked at the keypad. I'd completely forgotten about the security pad. We might have to spend the night in the vestibule at which point, upon finding our sleeping bodies wedged in, the landlady would be within her rights to evict us. Somehow Julius remembered the code, though, punched it in and the door to the stairs unlocked. Trying to get up to our second-floor sublet felt like the chase scene from *A Nightmare on Elm Street* with my feet feeling like they were being dragged under the carpet by gummy muck. Julius tugged and tugged on my coat as I held the rails and we made it to the sublet door.

Once inside, I told Julius he had to throw the joint away. *"This was a huge mistake,"* I said. I knew he was lying when he told me he'd discarded the joint and its plastic container on the way home. I was going to say that I hadn't seen a single garbage can the whole way home but then I became paranoid that he'd divorce me if I'd say this. I was also becoming preoccupied with the notion that Julius might put the joint in my luggage so that airport security would arrest me and throw me in jail, giving him all the more reason to divorce me.

"Julius!" I squealed, "I luuuuuuuvvvv you."

He reciprocated with a murmur and told me to get into bed.

From this point forward, scenes flickered in and out of my own powers of perception. I turned around and suddenly I was naked. And suddenly I was in pajamas. And suddenly I was under blankets. And suddenly I was pleading with Julius that we never do this again. And suddenly he's saying he feels all the tension pouring out of his shoulders. And suddenly he's going on about how he wants to do it again. And suddenly I'm shrieking *Nooooo*. And suddenly he's laughing and nodding. And suddenly the lights are off. There was no bridge between any of these sequences. I'd witness only a moment and then a gap and then another moment and then another gap and then another moment. The film reel in my mind had gone haywire.

I closed my eyes but remained awake and unable to sleep. I began to see *Felix the Cat* videos flickering on the insides of my eyelids. Felix's eyes and smile were as diabolical as Julius's had been when he'd said he could go in for another Greenhouse Hash Joint. Felix walked back and forth across a cartoon kitchen on his two spindly black legs, that shit-eating grin of his pushing further and further into the foreground for a close-up.

And then everything went black.

No images.

Nothing.

Yet I felt a Presence.

"God?" I said, "Is that you?"

The voice in the darkness said, "It is."

"God," I said, "I was raised a Catholic."

"I know that," God said.

"And not like *regular* Catholic," I said, "But *very* Catholic. I was an altar boy."

"Yes, I know," said God.

"God, I'm a Buddhist now," I said.

God said, "Fine by me."

"God," I said, "I'm a homosexual."

God said, "Thank you. I'm well-aware."

"My parents," I said, "They told me it's a mortal sin if I act on it. They said if you commit a mortal sin, you go to hell. I have acted on it, God. A lot. And I *do* act on it. Still. I'm even married to a man. See? He's right over there."

"Look, look," God said, "I know all this. I know *all* this. And let me just put you at ease here. I don't mind if you're a practicing homosexual."

"You don't?" I said.

"No," God said, "I don't."

"*Phew!*" I said with a chuckle.

"But I don't want you smoking hash again!"

"Okay," I said, "I'm way ahead of you on that one."

And then there was just a lot more darkness and a lot more wakefulness. Until, at some indeterminate point, I fell asleep.

When I finally woke up at about noon, I told Julius, "I know you have the Hash Joint. If you love me, you'll throw it out."

He balked. I stood my ground. He began going through his Gore-Tex coat pockets and throwing out Kleenex and receipts and cough-drop wrappers until finally he realized the jig was up. He could procrastinate no longer.

He handed me the plastic tube with a sigh.

Under the watchful eyes of God and Saturn, I threw the joint in the toilet and flushed it in a country where it's perfectly legal to have it on one's person.

I'd love to say it went down in that one flush but these European toilets just aren't built to flush something as thick and wide as a Greenhouse Hash Joint. It must have something to do with taxation.

Yet I wanted it gone. I wanted to signal to the universe that I could not be tempted again. Despite myself, I reached into the toilet water, picked up the sopping wet joint, broke it into little pieces and dropped it piece by piece into the toilet water.

Three flushes later, all the perfectly legal evidence had flushed down the toilet. I turned to the sink and literally scrubbed my hands of the whole ordeal with soft soap.

I cast my eyes to the ceiling.

I had a feeling that both God and Saturn were nodding.

N THE HOUSE

(*Kyle walks downstairs to hear "Compton's N the House" blasting*)

KYLE: Julius? You're cranking N.W.A.?

JULIUS: Yes. I enjoyed that biopic we saw yesterday so I downloaded the album. I have to say, I quite like it. It's a whole new experience for me. I'm going to listen to it on my way to the museum.

KYLE: What museum?

JULIUS: The Met. They're having an exhibit called *Warriors & Mothers: Epic Mbembe Art*. I'm going to play this in my headphones as I walk the galleries. There might be some . . . atavistic resonance. We'll see. Don't worry. I'll be home in time for dinner. (*Heads for door*) Peace out. (*Turns back*) I just learned that one.

PANGLOSS:
WORRY JAR, PART I

(The bathroom sink is clogged worse than ever, weeks after Kyle ritually burned the slips in his worry jar—the jar where he stores his worries for cosmic assistance—and then poured the ashes down the drain. Julius makes a last-ditch effort at Drano and plunging. The effort fails.)

JULIUS: Time to call a plumber and pay off his mortgage.

KYLE: Well, at least we learned something from this.

JULIUS: Oh, and what have *we* learned from this?

KYLE: That this is where worrying gets you.

JULIUS: Kyle. (*Deep breath*) Have you ever heard of Pangloss?

KYLE: No. Is he a good plumber?

FRENCH PHONE BY THE BED

(*Antique rotary phone rings and rattles like a Raisin Bran alarm clock next to Julius's side of the bed. Landline phone on computer desk down the hall blares like a prison-break siren. Kyle and Julius each open one bloodshot eye. Julius reaches limply over to the phone, picks it up, drops it back on the cradle and rolls back over.*)

KYLE: Did you just pick that up and hang it up?

JULIUS: (*annoyed*) Yes.

(*Julius buries his head back in the pillow.*)

KYLE: Well, why do we even have the landline in the first place?

JULIUS: (*snarls*) I don't know.

KYLE: Then why don't we get rid of it?

JULIUS: (*closes eyes tighter, pushes head deeper into pillow*) No.

KYLE: Why not?

JULIUS: It's irresponsible.

KYLE: And spending thirty bucks a month on a phone we don't use is responsible?

JULIUS: (*fading*) What if there's a fire?

KYLE: What, are we gonna run back in and hang up on the firemen?

JULIUS: Let me sleep.

KYLE: All that goddamn thing does is wake us up on the weekends. And four years ago, it was someone from the Romney campaign calling at the crack of dawn to get us to vote for Mitt and stop the spread of same-sex marriage.

JULIUS: (*yawns*) You know, it's at times like this that I wish I'd heard her out.

THE MEDIUM AT THE FIREMAN'S BALL

One of the PT guys, Brian, at my chiropractor's office is this barrel-chested Irish-American who lives with his girlfriend in Maspeth, Queens.

Brian told me that every year his girlfriend makes him go to the Fireman's Ball and every year the ball brings in a medium for entertainment.

This year, the medium cold-called from the middle of the banquet room, "Is there someone here whose grandmother died of a stroke?"

This didn't exactly narrow things down. Half the room's hands went up.

"She fell and hit her head?"

Brian's hand went up.

"It was in," the medium paused for a moment, closing his eyes and putting his fingertips to his temples, "A family restaurant?"

"Yes," Brian exulted, "It was in a Friendly's."

"On Long Island, right?"

"Right," Brian cheered.

"The doctors told her she was okay and sent her home," said the medium, "And she went to bed at her usual time?"

"Yes," said Brian, "And she didn't wake up. It was a brain lesion."

"Yes," said the medium, "That's what she's telling me too. And how long ago was this?"

"I don't know," said Brian, searching his memory banks, "I guess four years ago?"

"Yes," said the medium, "And you're one of nine children."

"Yes."

"Irish family?"

"Yes."

"Yes, that's what I'm getting," said the medium, "But one died?"

"Yes," said Brian, "At birth."

"Yes," said the medium, "That's what she's telling me too."

"Does she have a message for me?" Brian asked.

"She just wants you to know she's watching over you. That's all."

The PT studio sat in rapt silence.

"So what'd you say?" I said, breaking the silence.

Brian shrugged, "Uh, thanks."

Meghan, another PT therapist, said, "That's it? You didn't want to know anything else."

Brian shrugged again, "Well, he moved on to someone else."

"What'd he say to the other person?" I asked.

Brian said, "Oh I felt bad for the next guy. This medium guy said, 'Is there anyone here whose mother died two years ago?' And this one guy raised his hand. The medium said, 'And you didn't go visit her on her deathbed?' And the guy, he like nods. And the medium said, 'Yeah. She wants you to know . . . she hasn't forgotten about that.'"

GYMNOPEDIE

(Kyle wears nothing but a baby-blue exam gown, his legs in stirrups, as he discusses with Dr. M his impending cystoscopy, a bladder exam that requires sticking a tube with a small camera through his penis. Kyle clenches his jaw and attempts to shut his legs as Dr. M shows him the cysctoscope. Erik Satie's "Gymnopedie, No. 3" plays as part of the lilting-piano soundtrack that Dr. M uses to soothe male patients in what he affectionately refers to as The Chair.)

DR. M: Any more questions?

KYLE: I think you've prepped me. But no surprises?

DR. M: Well, I've given you the details of the procedure. Of course, nothing takes the place of experience, right? But beyond that, no, I don't think you should be expecting any surprises.

KYLE: (*huffs*) Okay, then.

DR. M: You look nervous. You shouldn't be. Your test results have been fine so far.

KYLE: No. It's just—like, for example, I'm not afraid of needles. But I still avert my eyes whenever I get a shot. That way it just feels like a little prick. No pun intended. (*Nervous laughter*) Of course, this time, you'll be the one feeling the little—

(*Door swings open. Giant woman swoops in out of nowhere.*)

NURSE: Hello!

DR. M: Oh, Kyle, meet Svetlana.

NURSE: Hello! (*Kyle hikes down gown*) Oh, look. He's trembling! Not the first to do that in The Chair.

DR. M: Svetlana will be assisting me. Is that a problem?

KYLE: (*motions doctor closer, whispers*) Well, it wouldn't be if her name were Sven!

DR. M: I'm sorry. I should have told you we wouldn't be alone.

NURSE: Shall I prepare the lidocaine swab?

KYLE: (*draws doctor closer, whispers again*) Just how "closely" will Svetlana be assisting?

(*Song draws to a violin-heavy crescendo*)

ASHES TO PASTE:
WORRY JAR, PART II

(Eduardo the handyman wrenches away at the bathroom sink.)

JULIUS: Eduardo told me that my using Drano probably made things worse. Drano can cut through food and hair, but it doesn't dissolve paper. It just makes paste out of it.

KYLE: Now, Julius, you mustn't blame yourself.

JULIUS: I don't.

KYLE: Well that's good. Because there's always the temptation to at times like this. Even I can't help feeling responsible.

JULIUS: Because you are.

KYLE: Thank you. I mean, I know I'm responsible as in "I pay my taxes," but I mean it more in the sense of... *culpable*.

JULIUS: You burned paper and poured it down the drain.

KYLE: Yes, but by then it was ash. Now, who ever heard of ashes making paste? You know, it's "ashes to ashes, dust to dust," not "Okay, he's cremated. Get the glue factory on the line. Tell 'em we got a big one for 'em."

COPENHAGEN

(*September 2014—Kyle and Julius enter taxi at Copenhagen Airport*)

DRIVER: Welcome to Copenhagen!

KYLE & JULIUS: Thank you!

DRIVER: You both like garlic?

JULIUS: Garlic?

DRIVER: Yes, garlic. Did you eat garlic on the plane?

KYLE: Well, there was some garlic in what we ate last night.

DRIVER: Yes, I can smell it.

KYLE: Oh, but we both brushed our teeth.

JULIUS: Yes, I brushed my teeth right after.

KYLE: So did I. And a few times after that. In fact, right before we landed. I'm a big brusher.

DRIVER: It doesn't matter how much you brush. Brushing is the least of it. You consume garlic, it gets in your skin. Once that happens, it does not matter how much you brush.

KYLE: (*whispers to Julius*) Do they work for tips in this country?

JULIUS: (*whispers to Kyle*) No, so he can speak freely.

KYLE: (*whispers*) Boy, imagine if one of us had had beans.—You'd think he'd start by saying, oh, "Is this your first time in Denmark?"

DRIVER: So, is it?

KYLE: (*to driver*) Sorry?

DRIVER: Is it your first time in Denmark?

HOME FROM DENMARK & A FUNERAL IN CHICAGO

(September 2014—On Kyle and Julius's second to last day in Denmark, Kyle received word that his brother Kent had died after drinking himself to death. Kyle and Julius flew to the funeral in Chicago and came right back home to New York. Kyle remembers Kent aloud to Julius in their bedroom.)

KYLE: But Kent…Kent was a funny guy.

(Without warning, the light bulb in the overhead lamp above the dresser goes out. Kyle and Julius watch as it proceeds to flicker back to life and then rises and rises and rises to full shining power.)

(**Author's Note:** Yes, this actually happened.)

CALCUTTA, OHIO

(*June 2014—Kyle and Julius sit quietly over appetizers at a French bistro on the Upper West Side, where they're seated next to a table of middle-age tourists, who are capping off their stay in Manhattan with yet another round of Manhattans.*)

JULIUS: Tell me honestly. Do you think I'm boring?

KYLE: No more than I am.

(*Woman at neighboring table lets out a shrill laugh and a snort.*)

KYLE: (*to Julius*) How was the philharmonic?

WOMAN: (*to her friends*) Did you know there are five towns in the United States called Calcutta?

JULIUS: (*to Kyle*) I've seen better Mendelssohn.

WOMAN: (*to her friends*) When I told this one New York woman we met I'm from Calcutta, she put her hand on my arm and said, "Oh, sweetie, the things you must have seen." (*Pauses to hyena-laugh, snorts, swigs her*

Manhattan) I said, "Well, I seen plenty of the sex trade in Calcutta, Ohio." (*To husband*) Hey, Rich. Trade ya my triangle for a trip to Bermuda. (*Roars, snorts, ice clinks in cocktail glasses.*)

KYLE: (*to Julius*) Well, I suppose even bad Mendelssohn is good.

JULIUS: (*to Kyle*) Oh, it wasn't bad. I've just seen better. What I'm holding out for are the Brahms concertos.

(*Table of tourists settles up bill, puts on coats. Man points to Julius's plate.*)

MAN: (*to Julius*) Those escargots?

JULIUS: Yes.

MAN: Better be careful. It'll make ya horny. (*Slaps Julius's back*) Ah-Hahahaha.

(*Tourists leave.*)

KYLE: So, *Upstairs, Downstairs* when we get back?

(*Enter Chorus.*)

CHORUS: You heard it yourselves, brave citizens of America. Mendelssohn, *Upstairs, Downstairs*, The Philharmonic. This is what you have to fear from the gathering storm of gay marriage. Transatlantic influences and the rampant viewing of PBS. Left unchecked, it might even cast its pall over the prim houses of Calcutta, Ohio.

APROPOS

(*Brooklyn—Big furry bald guy in a white tank-top undershirt smokes an unfiltered cigarette on his front steps as Kyle heads to the F train.*)

GUY: 'Scoose me.

KYLE: Yes?

GUY: What's "ah-pro-po" mean?

KYLE: Apropos? It refers to something that is appropriate to a given subject matter.

(*Guy takes a drag, looks at ground, considers.*)

GUY: So, like . . . How would I yooz it?

KYLE: Um, how about "Apropos of learning new words, 'apropos' is a good word to learn."

GUY: Ha! You can say it just like dat?

KYLE: Yeah. Yeah. Just like that . . .

GUY: Well, dat . . . dat…t'anks!

ALMODOVAR OR THE ANIMAL HOSPITAL?

(Early morning, vet's office. The Catalonian oncologist gives her take on Kyle's cat Giuseppe's medical records.)

VET: The C-T scan will naturally tell us more. We have reason to be optimistic. Up to now, his exams have been amazing. But how do we define amazing? Everything is subject to change, no? It's like when I discuss my sexuality. You know, I go back and forth. Am I bisexual? Am I pansexual? When it comes right down to it, I'm simply sexual.

KYLE: *(nodding)* So . . . you would recommend an ultrasound in addition to a C-T scan?

VET: Yes. That is what I'm trying to say.

K.ALI YUGA

(*Phone call*)

JULIUS: Hello?

KYLE: I fucked up. I fucked up! I fucked up!

JULIUS: What happened?

KYLE: I put my wallet in the laundry with my jeans.

JULIUS: No problem.

KYLE: Wait. There is a problem. My wallet is in the washing machine.

JULIUS: It's okay. Just stop the washer and take the wallet out of your jeans. (*Kyle does.*) Turn the washer back on. (*Kyle does.*) And go over to the paper towels. Take out your cash and your drivers license and your insurance, and if you can, take out your social security card. Put it all on the paper towel. Lay another paper towel over the contents of your wallet and press. (*Kyle does.*) Okay?

KYLE: No. It's not okay. This is terrible. This is terrible.

JULIUS: Kyyyyyle.

KYLE: Oh, could you be supportive please?

JULIUS: I am being supportive. I'm telling you what to do.

KYLE: Telling me what to do isn't being supportive. It's, it's . . . telling me what to do! This, this is upsetting. My credit cards were in there.

JULIUS: They'll still work.

KYLE: How do you know?

JULIUS: I was a compliance officer in the biggest banks for 25 years. I think I know.

KYLE: But these things demagnetize if you so much as breathe on them.

JULIUS: But they're water-resistant. You could wade through a swamp and they'd still work.

KYLE: And I did this. I did it to myself. It was all my fault.—I mean, this is one of those moments I can't even blame on you.

JULIUS: Yes, I know how difficult that must be for you.

KYLE: …or my parents.—Although, now that I think about it, they did raise me in such a way that—

JULIUS: *Kyle.*

KYLE: Eh, it was worth a shot.

JULIUS: So, does it look salvageable?

KYLE: Yeah. Even my social security card is pretty intact. I can still read the numbers on it. I've had it since I was 18.

JULIUS: Good. Is your wallet empty now?

KYLE: Yes.

JULIUS: Okay. Now just turn it over and let it stand on top of the paper towel until it dries.

(Kyle does.)

KYLE: Okay. But what do I do in the meantime? This was my only wallet.

JULIUS: Go to my dresser. You can use my green sports wallet. Nothing's in it right now.

(Kyle picks up green wallet but finds another.)

KYLE: Hey, wait! There's this other wallet. It's, I don't know, Monet's "Water Lillies" or something. Did you get this at MOMA?

JULIUS: No. I bought it in Paris.

KYLE: Paris! Wow. Can I use it?

JULIUS: If you're careful with it.—Oh my God! Look who I just said that to.

(Kyle walks back over to the paper towels on which the contents of his wallet are now drying. He's blithely placing various items into the Impressionist wallet.)

KYLE: Yeah, but I think there's a way to reframe all of this. I mean, you know that spiritual forum I'm involved in.

JULIUS: Yes, Kyle, I know all about your spiritual forum.

KYLE: Well, we were talking about that Hindu goddess Kali. She gets a bad rap for being Destroyer of Worlds. But, really, she's the essence of "out with the old, in with the new." She'll lay waste to anything that's corrupt or rotten or even just outmoded. And right now we're living in the age over which she presides.—Just yesterday she took out Steve Bannon.—Can't wait till she gets to Trump.

JULIUS: What does this have to do with your wallet?

KYLE: Well, in the forum, we were talking about how we were all going to make a practice out of clearing out everything we no longer need or use from our rooms, our closets, our drawers.—I thought, I'm way ahead of everyone because you and I already did all that with spring cleaning.—But then they said, "Clean out your wallets," and I thought, "When am I gonna get around to that?" Well! No time like the present!—Kali made sure of it. I mean, you should see what I've got on these paper towels. I have coffee cards from cafes that closed six years ago—

JULIUS: Wait, wait. Are you saying this is all the result of an ancient Hindu goddess throwing your wallet in the washing machine instead of you not being careful enough to check what was in your jeans before you did the wash?

KYLE: Well, if you want to get *prosaic* about it . . . But I like to look at these things from a more elevated vantage point.

JULIUS: Yeah, and in the process, you made off with a pretty snazzy new wallet.

TORMENTOR

(Kyle passes street preacher in front of Trump International Hotel, near Columbus Circle. Preacher is holding doomsday verse from Revelations on placard as the multitudes pass by.)

PREACHER: "And they shall be tormented day and night!"

KYLE: *(stops, looks preacher dead in the eye)* Why's that, honey? They gonna be havin' you over?

(Preacher stands dumbfounded. Kyle sashays away.)

ARISTOPHANES, REMEMBERED

(Kyle looks at the woman he's been sitting across from at the communal table at Konditori, the café where he writes.)

KYLE: Hey! I know you.

WOMAN: You do?

KYLE: Yes. You're from Louisiana. You were a classics major at University of Texas. Your brother is gay. And you have a beagle named Aristophanes.

WOMAN: Yes. How did you know all that?

KYLE: We talked once about three years ago. Right at this table, in fact.—How's Aristophanes?

WOMAN: Aristophanes is fine. Wow. You have a good memory.

KYLE: Not really. I just have an uneventful life—which is why I can remember things like beagles named Aristophanes.

TOUCHÉ

(Tuesday night—Kyle and Julius meet up at Puerto Alegre for a late-night supper.)

JULIUS: How was meditation class?

KYLE: Oh. We did something different after the dharma talk this time. There's this woman there who has this unearthly voice. And the teacher had her choose a dharma-related song from her repertoire and we all sang the refrain together: "Be kind!/Everyone is carrying a heavy burden./Be kind!/Everyone is carrying a heavy load." At first, we were all out of key. But, I don't know, something happened as we all started singing together. We kept singing the lines over and over again and we became this choir of angels. We all but levitated from all the, the, the LOVE in the room. It was, oh, it was . . .

(Kyle puts his hand over his heart and sighs.)

JULIUS: Sounds heartfelt.

KYLE: Oh, it was. It was.

(Kyle comes back down to earth. Takes a chip, dips it in salsa and eats it.)

KYLE: So that was my night.—How was fencing class?

JULIUS: Well, remember that French guy Jacques? The one who struts around like he's better than everyone? Well, he came at me with all this pas-de-deux and savoir-faire but I went in with the riposte and let's just say . . . he's lucky he had all that padding on.

A Party

JULIUS: Yes, Kyle, we're going to a party.

KYLE: But I don't like parties. You have to remember names and smile and say what you do and make it sound like something worth talking about. Can't I just stay in and watch *Grace & Frankie* with the cats?

JULIUS: No. We're going.

KYLE: You know Sartre said, "Hell is other people."

JULIUS: Yeah, and in case you haven't noticed, honey, this is hell. And you're gonna go up and you're gonna put on a smile and you're gonna ask the Devil's wife to dance if I have to . . . if I have to take away your iPhone.

KYLE: No. Not my iPhone. My Kindle's on there. I'm already on Book Four of that Norwegian navel-gazer's memoir. I was planning on finishing it by the punch bowl.

JULIUS: What page are you on now?

KYLE: One.

LATER AT THE PARTY

KYLE: Hi. I'm Kyle.

GUEST: I know. We talked about 10 minutes ago . . . for, like, half an hour.

KYLE: Oh! I'm sorry.—Do you know, I read in *Psychology Today* that we don't realize it, but the first thing we recognize each other by is our hair. So, even if I know you, if you've changed your hairstyle, I might think I don't know you.

GUEST: Really? Wow. That's interesting . . . Except I haven't changed my hairstyle in the past ten minutes.

KYLE: Well, now, you see, that . . . is a good point. They didn't really address that in the article.

THE MAN UPSTAIRS

(Kyle and Julius do a Sunday morning turn through David Sedaris.)

KYLE: I wish I could get this much material out of my own life.

JULIUS: You can. You just have to mine it.

KYLE: By now, I've said all I've got to say.

JULIUS: That's not true. Like, who was that guy who showed up at your mother's funeral? Your old neighbor, Mister . . . Klinkencumber?

KYLE: Mr. Klaustenberg.

JULIUS: Yes. He said you didn't like to wear shoes when you were little, so you'd just kick them off on the sidewalk and leave them there.

KYLE: But that's not a story. That's not even a tableau. It's a tidbit at best. Although the Klaustenbergs did have these two Collies, Carmel and Mitsy, and I used to go over there all the time to play with them. I went over there so much, Mrs. Klaustenberg gave me my own drawer in her kitchen to keep my crayons and coloring books in. After a while, I stopped ringing the doorbell. I'd just let myself in, color, play with the dogs. If Mrs. Klaustenberg happened to be passing by, maybe I'd say hi.

JULIUS: Maybe you'd say hi…in *her* kitchen?

KYLE: She didn't seem to mind. Oh, but one day . . . I went over, let myself in, and was just minding my own business.

JULIUS: Minding your own business, in *her* kitchen?

KYLE: When she came down in a robe and screamed. I mean, she screamed! I'd heard plenty of screaming by that point in my life, but this was something else. "Get Out, Kyle!" She lunged at me and I bolted out the kitchen door.

JULIUS: Okay, see? There's a story here. Then what happened?

KYLE: Well, then she ran to the front door and chased me down on the sidewalk.

JULIUS: She assaulted you?

KYLE: No. By now she'd changed her tune. She knew my next stop was going to be my mother and I was about to blab about what a bitch that Mrs. Klaustenberg was, so she attempted to buy my silence. She cooed, "Kyle, Carmel and Mitsy want to see you."

JULIUS: And did you go back?

KYLE: Of course.

JULIUS: She bought your silence?

KYLE: Right after she got the man she had upstairs down the backstairs and out of the house.

JULIUS: She had a man upstairs?

KYLE: Why else would she have been wearing a robe and screaming once she saw me in her kitchen?

JULIUS: That depends. Did she have a towel on her head?

KYLE: Wait, how'd you know?

JULIUS: Kyle, Mrs. Klaustenberg was probably just coming out of the shower and you startled her.

KYLE: Nah, I don't buy it.

JULIUS: Well, now, see? This is a story.

KYLE: Not unless she was in the shower with another man.

JULIUS: No, Kyle, it's enough to describe your laissez-faire treatment of her kitchen. And if you're going to publish it, change their names.

KYLE: I think Mrs. Klaustenberg is dead now.

JULIUS: Yeah, but what about Mr. Klaustenberg? Especially if you were to go with your implication that his wife was having an affair instead of innocently taking a shower, as the towel on her head would imply.

KYLE: Mr. Klaustenberg might be dead too.

JULIUS: He was alive last year.

KYLE: Yeah, but these people are dropping like Collies these days.

CAESAR FOR TWO

(*With tetchy Tuxedoed waiter at Grifone on the Upper East Side*)

JULIUS: So then, to reiterate, the specials are the squid and the seafood salad? Or is it the squid *in* the seafood salad?

WAITER: Look, I don't know anything about any *re-it-eratin'* but I'm gonna repeat what I just said. Are you listening? Okay. We have the squid. And . . . we have the seafood salad. Got it?

JULIUS: Oh, okay. Now I see.

WAITER: Great.

JULIUS: So then I'd like to have the Caesar but it says here it's for two.

WAITER: Eh, I can get 'em to make it for one.

JULIUS: You can? Great. Then I'll have the Caesar for one.

WAITER: Okay. Caesar for one. And for you, sir?

KYLE: I think I'll have the Caesar for one as well.

WAITER: That would make it the Caesar for *two*! Now look, you two, you need to either stop smoking weed or start smoking weed.

(Waiter walks off)

KYLE: See? New York's still got it.

THE COMEY LETTER

(October 28, 2016. Kyle and Julius see an Athol Fugard play at the Signature Theatre on the day that James Comey sent his infamous letter to congress.)

JULIUS: This election is killing me. I don't know how I'm even going to make it through the first week of November.

KYLE: Well, listen, let's just sit back, *relax* and enjoy this play about the South African uprising.

BAR BOULUD

(*Julius' Birthday at Bar Boulud, Manhattan*)

JULIUS: Vous êtes Parisien?

WAITER: (*In plain English*) No.

JULIUS: Êtes-vous français?

WAITER: No.

JULIUS: Mais votre accent! D'où êtes-vous?

WAITER: New Jersey.

TEMPLATE NOIR.

JULIUS: I think it's great that you're expanding your range.

KYLE: I can't. I can't write fiction. I can't!

JULIUS: Stop putting yourself down.

KYLE: It's so, derivative.

JULIUS: Well of course! It's going to be derivative. You're venturing into the noir genre. Hollywood established a template. But what counts is: Is it a good story?

KYLE: It's this courtroom scene. It's something we've heard a million times.

JULIUS: Well, let's take a look.

(Kyle hands Julius the pages.)

JULIUS: *(reads)* "The prosecuting attorney addressed the defendant, 'Ms. Brown, is Mr. Chambers correct in stating that you were working as a waitress in this cocktail bar?' Ms. Brown took a moment to compose herself, 'Yes. That much is true.'"

(Julius scratches his chin.)

JULIUS: Well, it's a first draft.

KYLE: Yes.

JULIUS: As an attorney, I do have to caution you against possible copyright infringements.

OLD CANARSIE

(*5:50 p.m.—Manhattan. After being at Animal Medical Center since dawn, a cat-carrier-toting Kyle calls his über driver to see where his car is. The über driver tells Kyle he's right outside. Bleary-eyed, Kyle walks up to a car that has its hazards on and climbs in the backseat.*)

KYLE: Hello.

DRIVER: 'Ey, Mac! What the hell you doin'! This ain't a cab.

KYLE: Oh, I'm sorry, sir. I thought you were my über driver. I'm so—

DRIVER: Hell's matta which ya?

KYLE: Sorry, sir. My mistake. (*Opens door to exit vehicle. Pauses.*) You know, it's funny. You called me Mac. That's old Brooklyn.

DRIVER: I know. I'm from ole Brooklyn! Canarsie. And I used to drive cabs in ole Brooklyn. But this ain't a cab and, unless you wanname to show you what the ole Brooklyn was really like, get the hell outta my backseat!

(Kyle exits vehicle)

A Rippling Cascade

JULIUS: Did you raise the curtains in the other room?

KYLE: Yes.

JULIUS: It was you then. Okay.

KYLE: What's the problem now?

JULIUS: Well, it's just . . . sometimes I wonder if you're really gay. I mean, they were all off-center and schlumpy. Oh, and look! You did these curtains too. (*Goes over, makes meticulous adjustments, stands at a distance framing curtains' new alignment with his hands*) You have to fluff them and let them fall in a rippling cascade.

KYLE: You know, sometimes I notice . . . you're really, really gay.

TREADMILL TONGLEN

KYLE: What I've found enormously helpful during these times is the Buddhist practice of tonglen. There is so much fear and so much of it *is* justified. So what do we do? In tonglen practice, we breathe in the despair, the anger, the rage, the division. We feel it fully so that we're not denying it. Then we breathe out peace or relief or compassion. Our minds become less clouded with the three poisons of greed, hatred and delusion, and our response to these events in our lives and in the world can become more skillful. It's the perfect prescription for times like these.

JULIUS: I'll have to try that.

(*Beat*)

KYLE: You know I have a pair of headphones that I wear on the treadmill. It has a metal bar connecting the headphones so that they don't fall off while I'm running. But I'm always afraid that the metal bar will rub my hair off and I'll end up bald.

(Julius nods solemnly)

JULIUS: Well, breathe in the fear of baldness and breathe out a full head of hair.

TRAIN GAUGE

KYLE: Okay. So, at this our twelfth year, we've reached an agreement. To improve on our conversational lulls, you'll try getting better at small talk and I'll try becoming more interested in arcane subjects that I have no exposure to in my daily life.

JULIUS: Agreed.

KYLE: Good.

JULIUS: Good.

KYLE: You know, I think we've really hit on something here. The floodgates might just open.

JULIUS: ——

KYLE: So . . .

JULIUS: ——

KYLE: What are you thinking?

JULIUS: (*sighs*) I was thinking, should Russia adopt the train gauge of western nations?

KYLE: ——

DR. GOLDBERG'S OFFICE

(Post-Election 2016, Kyle steps out into the gangway where Julius is counting a newborn shoal of koi in the koi pond to steady his nerves. A crushed Camel cigarette smolders beneath the toe of his shoe.)

KYLE: What the—?

JULIUS: I'm sorry. I . . . I smoked a cigarette, okay? I'm just really nervous.

KYLE: Wadda I look like? Jan Brady? Smoke 'em if you got 'em . . . at least for this week.

JULIUS: Listen, while you were having that emergency teleconference call with your meditation group, I called Dr. Goldberg to see if he can prescribe you clonazepam.— Look, I've been worried about you. You haven't been able to sleep or even think straight since last Tuesday. So I called him about it.

KYLE: What can Dr. Goldberg do about colonzapem? He's a GP not a shrink.

JULIUS: No, no. He's still licensed to prescribe it. Christina told me herself. She said, "Tell Mr. Smith that half of New York has been calling in for it. People who'd never even heard of it before the election are champing at the bit for it now. All lines are lit up from open to close of business day. Tell him we know these are scary times and I haven't slept all week either. But we'll be okay. I'll ask the doctor for the prescription and, in the meantime, please advise Mr. Smith not to exit the major cities. That way, he can ensure his safety."

KYLE: Wait, wait. Who's Christina?

JULIUS: The receptionist.

KYLE: The receptionist is advising patients on mental health and personal safety?

JULIUS: She's working in Dr. Goldberg's office. You know how it is on the Upper West Side. You have to wear more than one hat.

NON-SELF

KYLE: I moved to New York all those years ago so that one day I could be somebody. Now I spend my time in a meditation center where we have this guy walking around in a t-shirt that says, "30 years of meditation practice! And finally! A Nobody!"

JULIUS: Don't worry, Kyle. You'll get to where he is some day.

CATS AT THE DAWN OF THE TRUMP-RUSSIA ADMINISTRATION

(Unleashed by Petco, Brooklyn)

CLERK: Hi. May I help you with something?

KYLE: I don't know. Maybe. You see, our cat has outsmarted us.

CLERK: Let me guess—Pill Pockets.

KYLE: Yeah. How'd you know?

CLERK: You're the third one today. Actually, we usually average ten a day. They come in here saying, "My cat fell for the Pill Pockets for a while. Now he'll only eat around the pill."

KYLE: Yes! That's exactly what's happening. So, I dunno, do you have a tastier pill pocket? One that he'll just want to gobble up? Perhaps a more pungent one?

CLERK: I'm afraid not. And it's not for lack of trying on Tasty Treats' part. It's just . . . cats are becoming cagier.

KYLE: So, what do we do?

CLERK: Well, as a stopgap, there's this Alaskan salmon oil. But I'd be surprised if kitty doesn't turn up his nose before you're halfway through the bottle.

KYLE: *(takes it)* Well, it's better than nothing.

CLERK: Also, depending on your situation, you could hire a chef who'll serve up a fusion of feline and human food for your cat. We all know how cats like people food, am I right?

KYLE: No. We're not in any such "situation." Neither of us is related to Leona Helmsley—and even if we were, her estate went to the dogs—literally.

CLERK: Understood. Well, there have been some developments to help us "servantless cooks," as one Ms. Julia Child put it.

KYLE: And what are those?

CLERK: Well, one is a new culinary experience that my friend has designed. It's called "And Meow for the Main Course..." She's aiming to begin a 10-week class series next year.

KYLE: "And Meow for the Main Course...," you say?

CLERK: Catchy, right? And I knew her cats from before and after she started this new concept and, I have to tell you, the difference is Night and Day.

KYLE: Well, maybe after I finish grad school, I can take "And Meow for the Main Course." But for now I have two cats and one won't take his medicine and neither one will let us get any sleep. They keep running each other out of rooms in the middle of the night.

CLERK: (*nods*) It's post-election stress. Try a carton of Quiet Moments. It greatly reduces your cats' everyday anxiety and it's laced with Melatonin so that nighttime will become bedtime chez vous.

CONNOISSEUR, COME BACK TO EARTH

(*Wine Shop, 7th Av, Brooklyn*)

KYLE: Hello. We're having Mexican tonight and we need a wine to go with it.

CLERK: Wine? Mexican? We? Wait a minute. I know you. You with Julius. He send you?

KYLE: Yes.

CLERK: Well, tell him I said Veuve Cliquot ain't gonna cut it this time. He's eating Mexican, he's gotta get down and go earthy.

KYLE PINES FOR A MORE DIVERSE GENE POOL

After the White Supremacy-Tinged
Election of Donald J. Trump

(*Kyle's email dings*)

KYLE: Oh my God! It's 23 and Me! They have my test results! Now I'll finally find out that my ancestry isn't monolithic!

(*Frantically opens email*)

JULIUS: Well?

KYLE: Shit!

JULIUS: What's it say?

KYLE: Shit! This is the same shit Ancestry dot com says. It says 98.2% British & Irish and it doesn't even say which one.

JULIUS: Maybe you're both.

KYLE: Yeah, but I need hard evidence. I wanted to find out my ancestors went all the way back to Africa. Or even anywhere else in Europe. I was planning to wave this report high above my head and say to my mom and dad's ghosts, "See? We're not a hundred percent Irish. Read it and weep. We're more diverse than that."

JULIUS: I think your mother and father's ghosts can find better things to weep over in this world.

KYLE: The best I got is 0.2% Asian or Native American cos, y'know, they're the same thing, right? (*Looks closer*) Oh, wait! Woo-hoo!

JULIUS: What? What's it say?

KYLE: Netherlands!

JULIUS: Netherlands! Really?

KYLE: Oh no. Wait. No. It says Neanderthal. Goddamn dyslexia.

JULIUS: Neanderthal?

KYLE: Yeah. It says 4% of my DNA variants can be traced back to the Neanderthals.

JULIUS: Wow! Really? That's wonderful!

KYLE: Why's that wonderful?

JULIUS: Because that means you're not all Cro-Magnon.

KYLE: So?

JULIUS: Cro-Magnons were coarse and had terrible manners. The Neanderthals were the most civilized subspecies of archaic humans, though. They evolved from homo erectus.

KYLE: I guess that's where I get all my homo erections.

JULIUS: *(clasps hands, looks off in space)* Wow. I'm married to a Neanderthal.

AS HOPE PREPARES TO LEAVE OFFICE

KYLE: But I'll tell you why I think the two of us will be okay.

JULIUS: Why?

KYLE: Because I've got something going for me. A palm reader once showed me I have deep, straight lines in my palm. That means good fortune and spiritual protection. Plus, I have an Irish passport.

JULIUS: Yeah, and what do I have going for me?

KYLE: You're married to a guy with deep, straight lines in his palm and an Irish passport.

THANKSGIVING ANYWAY

(Thanksgiving 2016—The Little Owl, Greenwich Village)

JULIUS: Candlelight suits you. You look so chic in that turtleneck. And your skin is so radiant.

KYLE: (*hiding face*) Oh . . . go on.

JULIUS: (*trails fingertips on Kyle's hand*) What, I've never seen anyone grow so flustered when someone just says the truth.

KYLE: I have.

JULIUS: Who?

KYLE: Kellyanne Conway.

WIGGLE ROOM

(*In the Pilates studio with Brad, his Pilates instructor.*)

BRAD: Kyle, you have made MAJOR progress. I mean, before, you were a problem student. I was considering retiring.

KYLE: But Brad, you're only 36.

BRAD: Yes. And with a few more gray hairs since you walked in. Oh, but now you've not only gone from A to B. I'd say you've gone from A to a solid G.

KYLE: A "G"! Why, that's even better than an "F"!

BRAD: There's still a sticking point, though, Kyle. When I say, "Raise your right leg," you almost always raise your left leg. And vice versa.

KYLE: The thing is, Brad, since I'm facing you when you say it, I always think you mean *your* right, not mine.

BRAD: No, Kyle. Your right leg is your right leg, whether you're facing me or not. Your right leg will always be your right leg. It will never be your left leg.

KYLE: Well, let's say . . .

BRAD: I'm afraid there's no wiggle room on this one, Kyle.

JULIUS OFFERS ADDITIONAL TRAINING TO THE SUBSTITUTE CLEANING LADY

(Irena the cleaning lady is back in Poland looking after her elderly parents. Ewa, also from Poland, fills in for her. Julius gives Ewa a crash course in how he wants things done. He recaps his instructions as he walks down the stairs, one stair behind her with a hovering shadow.)

JULIUS: So, please remember that when you water the plant in back, you count backwards from 10. So, that's 10, 9, 8—

EWA: 7, 6—I got it.

JULIUS: Good. So then with the plant in the front, it's a little different. You count backwards from 7. It's a little tricky. So, it's backwards from 10 in the back room, but in the front room it's 7, 6—

EWA: 5, 4—I got it.

JULIUS: Okay, good. Now, would you like an almanac?

EWA: Almanac?

JULIUS: I love almanacs. And we have extra. Feel free. Or do you like calendars? I can give you calendars.

EWA: Calendar?

JULIUS: Yes. We have one from the Met, from their collection. And we have one with cats from Italy. Of course, the year is almost over but if you flip through, you'll find the cats are a bundle of mischievous fun, with names like Luigi and Bomboloni!

EWA: No, no. Thank you, mister. I no need calendar. I only need, how do you say . . . space.

DUCK SOUP

(*Kyle is in the shower*)

JULIUS: (*shouts from other room*) Kyle, I'm checking our order cart. It says you added two items: The Marx Brothers' *Duck Soup* and *Spiritual Progress Through Past Life Regression*. Is that right?

KYLE: (*shouts from shower*) Yes, that's right.

JULIUS: (*murmurs*) Only in this house could that be right.

WATER BUFFALOS

(Over the Christmas holidays, Kyle and Julius take a long-awaited trip to Sri Lanka and try to pull themselves together after the 2016 presidential election. They drive through a game park.)

KYLE: Hey, look! Water buffalos.

JULIUS: Where? (*Sees*) Oh yeah.

KYLE: They're, um, they're . . . doing that thing I always do . . .

JULIUS: Wallowing?

KYLE: That's it!

A SACKFUL OF GOLD

Nuwara Eliya, Sri Lanka

Yesterday we were at a buffet, sitting next to a family who was visiting from Mumbai. The younger brother, who couldn't have been more than four, spilled his water. As the father went to fetch napkins, the older brother, who couldn't have been more than six, stood up in his chair and dressed down the younger brother: "Do you not know that water is more valuable to a thirsty man than a sackful of gold! A sackful of gold! Do you want to be responsible for dropping a sackful of gold!" The 4-year-old brother looked down shame-faced as his 6-year-old brother chastised him with words that he seemed to be channeling from a 600-year-old storybook. If only American adults would chastise each other with such gravitas.

MONKEYS MATE OUTSIDE THE DUMBULLA CAVE TEMPLE IN SRI LANKA

When the female monkey's face is red, it means it's mating season. The male monkey was petting, hugging, and kissing her. It was the cutest display of courtship I'd ever seen. At least it was until he turned her upside-down, picked something out of her butt and ate it. It didn't kill the mood for her but it did for me.

COUNTER ACTIVE

(Christmas Day, under the breakfast mistletoe, Anuradhapura, Sri Lanka.)

JULIUS: It doesn't feel like Christmas.

KYLE: That's alright. Just open to the moment. Let it be whatever it is.

JULIUS: I left your present at home.

KYLE: Eh. That's okay. What was it?

JULIUS: A tray to put your malaria pills on.

KYLE: Wow. Warm my cockles, why dontcha.

JULIUS: At least I'm here to make sure you're taking them. Malaria is a terrible thing.

KYLE: It has its upside.

JULIUS: And what's that?

KYLE: If there's ever anything you don't want to do, you just go, "Sorry. Can't. Got malaria."

JULIUS: Yes, for you, malaria would be the gift that keeps on giving.

KYLE: But you keep forcing these counteractive meds down my throat.

A MAN LIVES ON A HIGH-SCHOOL TEACHER'S SALARY IN EUROPE

(*Kyle makes friends with a man named Dinesh and his family in Galle, Sri Lanka.*)

KYLE: So you guys get a lot of our stuff! Do you get *Breaking Bad*?

DINESH: Oh yes. Have you seen the European version of *Breaking Bad*?

KYLE: There's a European version of *Breaking Bad*?

DINESH: Yes. A man living on a high-school teacher's salary in Europe finds out he has cancer. So he goes to National Health Services, gets his treatments for free and goes home.

NEW YEARS EVE, SRI LANKA

KYLE: On New Years Day, we should do what we did at the Hindu temple. We can hold coconuts and meditate. And as we do, we can pour all the hellish-ness of 2016 into the coconuts. Once we're done doing that, we'll smash them on the concrete and release all the 2016 toxins while invoking the most positive energies for 2017.

JULIUS: Well, we can do that, sure. But we have to plan this.

KYLE: Plan it? I just told you the plan.

JULIUS: It's not that simple. First we have to acquire the coconuts.

KYLE: Acquire? There's a coconut stand every five miles. We'll pull over. Quid pro quo. Done.

JULIUS: Done? There are exchange rates.

KYLE: They're fifty cents each. I think we can afford them.

JULIUS: It's not a matter of afford. It's a matter of conversion. You've got to stop thinking in terms of cents and start thinking in terms of rupees. Otherwise they'll fleece you skin and bone.

KYLE: Oh God! You know, this is supposed to be a rite of liberation. Can't you just go with the prajna, the chi?

JULIUS: Once again, it's not that simple. Coconuts don't just grow on trees.

(*Beat*)

KYLE: Yes they do!

THE FRANKFURT SCHOOL

(Julius watches the morning light off the hotel terrace in Galle, Sri Lanka.)

KYLE: You know, it's too bad our Wi-Fi signal doesn't extend to our kitchen. Because then we could watch *The Man in the High Castle* online while eating dinner. I've never seen it but I hear it's about what it would have been like if America had become a fascist state in the 1940s. It could give us real insight into our times. Of course, maybe not. The world has changed so much since then. They didn't have Internet technology or social media as an arm of a ministry of propaganda. You know, I was just reading something about how the Frankfurt School saw Trump coming all the way back in the 1920s.(*Looks at Julius*) Hello! Did you hear anything I just said?

JULIUS: Yes! I'm listening.

KYLE: Okay. What did I say?

JULIUS: A man in a high castle in Frankfurt gives us insights into fascism by sending messages over the Internet.

THE ZAFTIG HILDEGARD

(After falling asleep to the same past-life regression CD, night after night, Julius and Kyle finally discover how they met in a previous incarnation.)

JULIUS: So that was you? In 19th Century Düsseldorf?

KYLE: Yep. I was the zaftig Hildegard from the red bordello, just outside the city limits.

JULIUS: And I was a financier.

KYLE: The richest man in town. And you sure kept me in satin and snowdrops.

JULIUS: It was love. But it couldn't be. My social rank forbade it.

KYLE: Um, don't flatter yourself, honey. The truth is, I had to send *you* away.

JULIUS: Send *me* away?

KYLE: Before closing her eyes to this world, my bordello mother told me never to marry a client who had a better time flouncing around the parlor in my garters and corsets than I did. I'm sorry, my dear, but I'd seen you do it one too many times.

JULIUS: But you looked crestfallen when I walked away forever, with that limp. You'd tear up when we'd pass as strangers in the village square.

KYLE: Um, ever hear of 'faking it'? After so many years of you trying on my dresses and lingerie, I began to save a fortune with the laundry girl.—But here we are, the two of us, three centuries later.

TWILIGHT WALK THROUGH MONTREAL'S OLD CITY

(April 2017)

JULIUS: So, just theoretically: if they were gay and you were single, which one would you sleep with? Bernie Sanders or Justin Trudeau?

KYLE: Well, Justin Trudeau.

JULIUS: Of course, because he's young and cute.

KYLE: No, because he could get me a Canadian passport.

ICE BLOCK

JULIUS: Wow. So you dated a lot of actors.

KYLE: It was kinda my thing for a while.

JULIUS: But Ian was the smartest?

KYLE: Oh, he was brilliant. Do you know, he told me that this one time he was on tour with his company during a heat wave in, um, I don't know, somewhere in the Deep South. They were put up in an old army barracks with no A/C.

JULIUS: This is starting to sound a lot like *Biloxi Blues*.

KYLE: According to Ian, everyone around him was queening out. But Ian found a tray of ice cubes in the kitchen freezer, which he put in a bowl and set next to a fan that was in the window. And for the whole day, everyone who huddled around the bowl felt like they had air conditioning. I asked him, "How did you come up with something so clever?" He said, "I saw it done once in a documentary about people recovering from malaria."

JULIUS: Well, unless you have another tray of ice cubes ready to go within 15 or 20 minutes tops, that little strategy of his would produce nothing more than a big bowl of water and maybe the slightest wisp of an arctic breeze for those overheated thespians he was running around with. It would have been far better to put a block of ice on a tray like they do for malaria patients in the Congo, in Kasai, with immediate provisions of backup ice blocks. If he's so clever, why didn't he think of that?

KYLE: He wasn't off-book yet. Even geniuses only have so much mental space.

JULIUS: Well a true genius would have a contingency plan in place even if they don't know their lines yet.

KYLE: Relax, Julius. I'm off actors. Compliance officers are more my scene now.

EPIPHANY

(*Over the phone*)

KYLE: You sound bummed.

JULIUS: No.

KYLE: You sound it.

JULIUS: Well, that's just how I sound. Doesn't mean that's how I am. It's kind of like that joke about the horse that walks into the bar.

KYLE: Why did the horse walk into the bar?

JULIUS: Why?

KYLE: No. That's what I'm asking you.

JULIUS: Oh, you mean, why did the horse walk into the bar in the joke? I don't know. He just did.

KYLE: Oh, so this is like "a guy walks into a bar" joke but it's a horse, not a guy.

JULIUS: Right.

KYLE: So what happened after the horse walked into the bar?

JULIUS: Well, the bartender said, "Why the long face?"

KYLE: And what'd the horse say?

JULIUS: The horse didn't say anything. That's the punchline.

KYLE: The punchline is that the horse didn't say anything?

JULIUS: No. The punchline is that the horse had a long face.

KYLE: But why did the horse have a long face?

JULIUS: (*deep breath*) Because, Kyle, horses have long faces.

KYLE: Oh. (*pause, epiphany*) Oh!

TASTES CHANGE

(Redecorating before a dinner party, Julius replaces a lovely impressionistic lacquered oil painting from China with an unattractive American painter's self-portrait of himself in the shower. The portrait features the painter carrying what appears to be a tube of toothpaste and a toothbrush like chewing bones in his mouth, though closer inspection reveals that his mouth is actually stuffed with his paint tube and paintbrush. Kyle reacts.)

KYLE: No. No. And, um . . . no.

JULIUS: Maybe?

KYLE: Maybe? Maybe we can burn it out back before the guests come, maybe. Seriously, you used to be this paragon of good taste. What the hell happened?

JULIUS: I think it's bold and shocking.

KYLE: Well I have one in the basement of a big, sweaty guy on the toilet. I got it from the BFA show at SVA. Maybe we can find a spot for it in the dining room.

JULIUS: Sure. It could be our own version of Rodin's *The Thinker*.

KYLE: Yes, except this one's from an undergrad named Rodent and his painting's called *The Stinker*.

IN A KORNFIELD WITH RUDY GIULIANI

(Waiting room. Kyle picks Julius up from a medical procedure that required heavy sedation.)

KYLE: So you wanna hear about my day?—Okay, so, with you being under sedation and all, I figured I'd go for a nice lunch and read Jack Kornfield's new book, *No Time Like the Present*. It's all about cultivating present-moment awareness.

(Julius slumps over)

KYLE: Excuse me. Are you listening?

JULIUS: *(coming to)* Yes. Precious moments . . .

KYLE: And inner peace. And I thought, what could be a nicer place to read this but this one little Italian joint I found tucked away on 44th St. So I went in and propped open my Kindle and I'm really settling in and . . . oh, you might not have seen this on the news, being unconscious and all . . . but I look up at the TV that they have over the corner table and there's footage of the police shooting water cannons at the G-20 protesters in Hamburg and Cologne.

JULIUS: (*droning*) I need to stop off and buy cologne.

KYLE: And the newscasters call this "crowd control." Crowd control? Okay, so water cannons are the new "crowd control." So I get all upset but I'm reading Jack Kornfield so it'd be really stupid for me to lose my shit right now. So I got to the men's room and I splash cold water all over my face and stand stock-still and repeated some *metta* phrases until this guy who looked like James Gandalfini walks in and looks over his shoulder at me while he's using the urinal.

JULIUS: They do sell good cologne on 5th Avenue.

KYLE: So I walk out and on my way back, I catch sight of all the framed photos in the hallway. Autographed photos of people who've visited the restaurant. And who do you think is up there?

JULIUS: Not Helmut Kohl.

KYLE: Rudy Giuliani. Donald Trump. Pat Sajak. The Trifecta. Of course, Rosie O'Donnell's was up there too, I guess for balance, but that's not the point. Suddenly this corridor becomes a chamber of horrors. I mean, they really should show people to the hallway to the men's room before they take their money. Except then I saw what I'd missed when I'd walked in the front door. Right above the hostess's stand: a caricature of Rudy Giuliani stabbing his fascist finger into the foreground and saying, "I'm Makin'

New Yawk Safe." And here I am on my second Chianti and there's no way around paying these enablers.

JULIUS: *(slightly lucid)* Kyle, didn't your dharma teacher warn you against indulging in tension and drama?

KYLE: I'm almost done. So I pick up Jack Kornfield thinking he might have something to say for a moment like this. And then these tourists from Kentucky--I don't know why they were in this part of town, but there they were, sitting in outfits that nobody's worn since Suzanne Sugarbaker in *Designing Women*, and they're looking at the news and one of them says, "These hooligans with their socialism are spitting in the face of the country that saved them from Hitler." I was gonna lose my shit but I was reading Jack Kornfield so I just asked for the check.

JULIUS: *(going under)* Kyle, not everyone sees the world through the same prism. Not everyone is a gay man living in Brooklyn.

KYLE: I know. I know. And I have no idea how there can ever be such thing as an "enlightened society" until everyone is.

PROTÉGÉ

KYLE: How was your meditation?

JULIUS: Good.

KYLE: You're really sticking with it. I'm so impressed.

JULIUS: I feel like I'm turning into you.

KYLE: Don't be silly. The more you meditate, the more you become like yourself. Now, what we need to do is get you on one of those ten-day Vipassana retreats at IMS.

JULIUS: I feel like you're *trying* to turn me into you.

KYLE: Julius, do we have to argue about this? You know you have your first consultation with the astrologer in ten minutes. You have to be centered.

TECHNICAL ASSISTANCE WITH THE DEAD

(Apple Store, Williamsburg, Brooklyn)

JULIUS: A startup in San Francisco is developing an Artificial Intelligence program that will allow you to speak to the dead, all based on an aggregate of their Cloud data.

KYLE: That's disgraceful. When will we learn that the key to a good life is learning how to let go?

JULIUS: I think we should invest in that program.

KYLE: Why?

JULIUS: Because I'm afraid you won't be able to function in this world if something were to happen to me. I'm planning on leaving behind *extensive* notes in the Cloud.

KYLE: Why?

JULIUS: Well, for one thing, you called the Bluetooth Ear Pods "those thingamadoodles." You pointed to your ears and asked the sales associate for "those thingamadoodles."

You even twirled your fingers. I'm creating files, and files, full of notes.

(*Beat*)

KYLE: (*cocked head*) Blue . . . ?

JULIUS: Bluetooth, Kyle. Bluetooth.

DOR

(Kyle interviews a Romanian translator who's wistfully swilling a vodka-tonic at KGB Bar in Manhattan.)

TRANSLATOR: So that's the thing about the word *Dor*. An English-Romanian dictionary will tell you it means "longing," but that's not it. That's not it at all. It's more than longing. *Dor* is a longing for something that's lost and that you can never get back. A longing for something that is lost to you forever. Irretrievably. Do you understand?

KYLE: Yes.

TRANSLATOR: Now I ask you, is there an English equivalent for *Dor*?

KYLE: *(weakly)* Well . . . "nostalgia."

TRANSLATOR: Ha! Nostalgia? Nostalgia is an Elvis Presley song. Nostalgia is not *Dor*! Nostalgia is wiping off a dirty window in a 1960s movie and seeing a scene from a 1940s dancehall. It is not *Dor*! Nostalgia is buying tchotchkes at a vintage shop. Nostalgia is not the experience of being eviscerated and having your guts fed to ravenous curs and jackals while you bleed in the gutter--only the curs and the jackals don't eat your heart. No. Your heart rips away, ever so slowly, from your very being, and of its own accord, as you lay praying for death. That . . . that is *Dor*!

(*Beat*)

KYLE: Wow! So I guess you had to use an endnote when you hit that word.

TRANSLATOR: (*slugs back drink*) I had no choice. There simply was no English equivalent. And I searched high and low. It's a translator's life. Searching high and low. High and low for that ineffable feeling. (*Takes a sip and a breath*) This morning I was listening to Brahms on the bus to work and I marveled at how he is able to capture in music that unquenchable thirst for an unattainable object of desire. (*Slugs back the remainder of his drink*) I even wrote that very phrase on my phone when it came to me. (*Shows it*) See? "That unquenchable thirst for an unattainable object of desire." (*Puts down phone*) You can express that feeling in music but not in words. I know no one word for it. And this is the life of a translator. (*Hangs his head*) This is the life of a translator. Now, I ask you, have you ever had this?

KYLE: Had what?

TRANSLATOR: What I've been describing! Haven't you been listening? "That unquenchable thirst for an unattainable object of desire." Have you ever had this?

KYLE: Er . . . Yes!

TRANSLATOR: Then what is it? What is "that unquenchable thirst" for in your own life? What is your "unattainable object of desire"? What is your unquenchable thirst for!

KYLE: A . . . a publishing contract.

TRANSLATOR: Yes. Me too.

THE LEOPARD AT DES ARTISTES

(Kyle and Julius sit at the bar before their table is ready at The Leopard at Des Artistes restaurant in Manhattan.)

BARMAID: Oh, so I see you've had a look at our Celebratory 1920s Cocktail Menu.

KYLE: Yes. I'll have the Sidecar.

JULIUS: I'll have the Fountain of Youth.

BARMAID: Usually it's the ones who order the Sidecar who come back for the Fountain of Youth.

THE POST-STRUCTURALIST MAFIA

JULIUS: Every day I wake up and look at this country and think, "How? How did this happen?"

KYLE: I still can't call it genius. That bumbling fool act of his, it's not an act. That's who he is.

JULIUS: But then how did he pull it off?

KYLE: It's not genius. He encourages people's basest, most puerile impulses. And they like that. And I refuse to call it genius.

JULIUS: But then how come he won?

KYLE: He scapegoats. Gives easy answers to complex problems. He exploits our collective shadow. He's like Don Corleone's mafia. He sees the worst in us and makes it an offer it can't refuse.

JULIUS: And our side?

KYLE: Well, especially to the heartland, our side's the poststructuralist mafia.

JULIUS: The poststructuralist mafia?

KYLE: Yeah. We make them an offer they can't understand.

SLACK.

(Julius has left the banking world in New York to accept a job as Chief Compliance and Risk Officer for a startup in San Francisco. Hanging up his suit for good, he puts his casuals on one leg at a time like everyone else and starts posting on social media like everyone else. Back in New York, he shows Kyle some of his new moves.)

JULIUS: So, read this post that I sent to my team on Slack.

KYLE: Slack?

JULIUS: It's an app we all post on.

KYLE: Well! Look at you posting on the app called Slack!

JULIUS: Yes but I'm not sure I have all the lingo down. Here, read what I posted this morning. Tell me what you think?

KYLE: *(Scans post)* Hmmm . . .

JULIUS: What?

KYLE: Well, you say here, and I quote: "Though I have not pride of authorship." That's what it says. It says: "Though I have not pride of authorship."

JULIUS: Too old-fashioned?

KYLE: It's more than old-fashioned. I think Shakespeare actually said that at a production meeting at The Globe.

THE LOWER HAIGHT

(Kyle arrives in San Francisco. Julius takes him to the neighborhood where they're going to be living.)

KYLE: I just thought I looked younger. That's all.

JULIUS: Kyle, the Lyft driver said you look young. He said it!

KYLE: No, he said, "A lot of young people are moving into that neighborhood."

JULIUS: Yes, he said you'll like it there. A lot of young people are moving in.

KYLE: Yeah, but when I asked him how old he thinks I am—

JULIUS: He gave a correct estimate of your age.

KYLE: Yeah, but I just don't think he meant "between 40 and death" as a compliment.

THE SNAKE PIT

(*Back in New York. The reality of Kyle's upcoming move to San Francisco has hit him hard. He's breathing into a paper bag.*)

JULIUS: Kyle, what . . . ?

KYLE: (*removes bag from mouth*) It's an oldie but goody.

JULIUS: Did you meditate?

KYLE: It didn't work.

(*Goes back to bag*)

JULIUS: Clonazepam?

KYLE: I'm tapped out.

              (*Takes deep inhale*)

JULIUS: Was it the I Ching?

KYLE: Said scary stuff.

           (*Breathes in and out in paper bag*)

JULIUS: Oh, the I Ching's so ambiguous. It'll say, "The sparrow meets the dragon that plays the lute for the periwinkle goose," and all of a sudden you're wondering if you should check yourself into Bellevue and live out the rest of your days in a rubber room.

KYLE: Just tell me everything's going to be okay.

JULIUS: Everything's gonna be fine. It's just that right now we're like an engorged snake.

>   (*Julius circles his arms and holds them out wide in front of him, simulating the belly of a goblin who's just gobbled up a town-hall meeting.*)

KYLE: An engorged snake? What are you talking about?

JULIUS: Oh, a periwinkle goose makes all the sense in the world to you but throw in an engorged snake and you're looking at me like I'm the one who should be carted off to Bellevue.

KYLE: How are we like an engorged snake?

JULIUS: Well you know how a snake will consume a whole pig and afterwards (*puts out arms again*) it just sort of tries to slug along on its belly with the pig's hoofs pushing against its innards. Its stomach is painfully distended. But then! It digests the pig and life goes on. For the snake anyway. So that's how we're going to be for the first year.

>   (*Kyle does a few more deep breathing exercises into the paper bag.*)

KYLE: It's a good thing you're not the hospital chaplain at Bellevue.

JULIUS: Why do you say that?

KYLE: Because you have the bedside manner of a lobotomist.

THE LONDON PSYCHIC

Oh, NYC! What'll I do when I no longer have you to eavesdrop on?

Two older middle-age women with brawny Queens accents were talking on the downtown F about a psychic one of them went to see on her first-ever trip to London:

"And she says I'm a real thinker type."

"A *thinker* type?"

"Yeah," said the woman, tapping her temple, "She says I'm very mental."

EXEUNT

The biggest bridge club on the eastern seaboard is conveniently located one floor down from my chiropractor in the E50s. Every time we approach the 14th Floor, the retirees who ride the elevator with me lurch forward like roulette addicts in Vegas.

On my last day in New York, I went to visit my chiropractor one last time and overheard two old ladies from the bridge club having the following conversation.

"What happened to Murray? He doesn't come anymore."

"Suspended."

"They suspended him? What for?"

"He brought in one of his old decks."

"So what? I brought in one of my own decks last week. In fact, it belonged to my mother. I brought it to memorialize her on her birthday. And when Joan came around and asked me about it, I told her and she said, 'Oh, that's so lovely.'"

"Yeah, well, these weren't your mother's playing cards, Sylvia, and they weren't lovely. Let's just put it that way."

"You mean . . . ?"

"Yeah, *those* kinda playing cards. The kind he used to play poker with, with his buddies back when they were bachelors."

"Oh. But Joan didn't used to suspend anybody over that. She'd just let them off with a warning."

"Well, Sylvia, this was probably Murray's sixth warning so he's suspended six months."

"Oh. Well when you're Murray's age, you're not guaranteed six months."

"Yeah, now he's got all day to look at those cards. Can't be good for his heart."

"I'll drop by his place with a roast this weekend."

The elevator door opened.

They trundled over to the coatroom.

I left for San Francisco the next morning with this and so many other scenes from our life in New York playing in my mind.

THE THEATRE LOFTS:
A THREE-RING EPILOGUE

SINKING IN

(*Kyle's ADD goes haywire as he tries to coordinate repairs and renovations with Vince the handyman in the San Francisco apartment. Finally, Kyle gets Julius on the phone from NYC.*)

KYLE: (*on speakerphone*) Now Vince is asking what he's supposed to do after he takes the downstairs sink out to make room for the shelves?

JULIUS: Tell him to just throw it out.

KYLE: How do you throw out a sink?

JULIUS: You throw it out.

KYLE: What, like heave it over the neighbor's fence? We haven't even met them yet.

JULIUS: I'm sure Vince knows places.

KYLE: What makes you think he'll do us any favors?

JULIUS: How much is in your wallet?

KYLE: A few twenties.

JULIUS: Perfect!

KYLE: You're not suggesting . . .

JULIUS: Kyle, what did we learn yesterday about the subtle art of bribery?

(*Memory-fade into the day before. The Sears delivery guy talks to Kyle in the laundry room while Julius is on speakerphone.*)

SEARS: I'm sorry but we have a problem. You ordered an electric dryer but you only have gas-dryer capabilities. I can't hook this up.

JULIUS: (*on speakerphone*) Oh. The building manager said it was electric.

SEARS: Well, it's not.

JULIUS: Oh, I guess I'll have to reorder. But before I do, can you at least unstack the washer and dryer that's already there?

SEARS: Unstack?

JULIUS: Yeah. See how the dryer is on top of the washer? We need them side-by-side so we can put up shelves.

SEARS: Sir, I can't. I'm only authorized to install and return your merchandise. Now, you can go online and . . .

JULIUS: For a hundred bucks?

SEARS: (*pauses, calls guy in truck*) Hey, Lennie. Get off your can and help me unstack these things, will ya?

JULIUS: (*to Kyle, over speakerphone*) Kyle, would you mind going to the ATM?

>   (*The scene returns to the present moment as Kyle ends his contemplation.*)

JULIUS: (*over speakerphone*) So . . . ?

(*Kyle walks over to the top of the stairs as if under a hex.*)

KYLE: Hey, Vince!

VINCE: (*offstage*) Yeah?

KYLE: There's sixty bucks in it for ya if ya make like we never saw that sink before!

VINCE: (*offstage*) Okay!

>   (*Beat*)

JULIUS: (*speakerphone*) Now, I'm going to ask you this again, Kyle: What country do we live in?

KYLE: *(grumbles)* America.

JULIUS: (*speakerphone)* I'm sorry. There seems to be a little static on my end. What country was that again?

KYLE: The United States of America!

BOWLS

(*Today is the day that Kyle and Julius's furniture comes in from New York. Kyle and Julius are packing up to check into a hotel downtown with their cat Giuseppe. It's another day of working around rugged, masculine movers as Kyle washes Giuseppe's dishes in the sink.*)

JULIUS: (*offstage*) Kyle, we need to go!

KYLE: (*yells*) Okay! I just want to wash his bowls first.

(*A mover in a Harley-Davidson t-shirt hears this and looks at Kyle, startled.*)

KYLE: (*to mover*) I said "bowls." And I was talking about a cat.

THE THEATRE LOFTS

Julius got a job with a startup in San Francisco so we're going to be living out west for at least a few years. In the meantime, we'll be renting out our place in Brooklyn, the one with the cockloft. At first, I didn't take this news well. New York is the land of snappy dialogues and I didn't know if I'd be able to still have them, much less transcribe them, if we were to leave.

Yet we have since moved into a building in the Lower Haight called The Theatre Lofts. My next-door neighbor Kelsey, who moved here last summer from Chelsea, said, "Don't worry about leaving your cockloft. You'll find plenty of drama right here in The Theatre Lofts."

I'm happy to report that I'm starting to like this new city.

One of the many great things about San Francisco is how conveniently located everything is. For instance, in the Castro, Moby Dick (a bar) is right across the street from Hand Job (a spa).

I'm thinking a sequel for *Cockloft* may already be writing itself.

AFTERWORD:
MINI-PIZZA BAGELS AND THE REAL MASTERPIECE

(Author's Note: Just in case you're wondering how Cockloft *came to be* Cockloft, *the following is my process paper from grad school, where the book you're holding in your hands was my thesis. Around the age of 40, I was having a terrible time coming up with a viable book concept, so at 41, I bit the bullet and did something I thought I'd never do—I enrolled in an MFA program. More specifically, the MFA Program for Creative Writing and Literary Translation at City University of New York, Queens College. That did the trick. Keep reading...)*

Of all the quotable quotes that Leonard Cohen left us prior to his death in 2016, the following might just be his most important—at least for the purposes of my thesis and indeed of my entire graduate education:

> I found that things became a lot easier when I no longer expected to win. You abandon your masterpiece and sink

into the real masterpiece. (Liebovitz 220)

As a deeply contemplative singer-songwriter and one-time Zen monk, Cohen recognized that the "real masterpiece" is life itself—in all its madness, mundaneness and mystery. My thesis, *Cockloft: Scenes from a Gay Marriage*, is my own attempt to do what Cohen suggests he'd begun doing at a certain point in his musical career—abandoning my own insistence that I write great masterpieces, something I've found myself woefully incapable of doing, and instead focusing on mindfully capturing the small, evanescent moments that comprise my own real life and the life that I share with my husband Julius. Ironically, ever since I began this lower-stakes way of writing, I have found myself on a creative tear, spontaneously producing vignettes and personal essays that my readers have found far more enjoyable and authentic than any of my past attempts at masterworks, which more often than not left me utterly creatively stymied.

I owe a tremendous debt of gratitude to Richard Schotter for seeing the potential in this collection. In my first semester of this program, I took his playwriting workshop. During the first few weeks, I turned in a couple of one-acts that met with a lukewarm reception from my fellow workshop participants. What can I say? I bombed. Yet one night, when I was coming home from class feeling like a total failure, I was thunderstruck by the most obvious revelation: Why not turn in the dialogues and scenes that I'd been recording from my relationship with Julius? After all, I'd been entertaining my Facebook friends with them for years. I figured they might at least give the class a chuckle.

I ran home, wolfed down my dinner, grabbed my laptop and left Julius to do the dishes as I went about copying and pasting all the dialogues and vignettes from my Facebook timeline into a Word doc. By the end of the week, I'd amassed a whole sheaf of material, which I emailed to the class for review. At first, I was afraid that Richard wouldn't accept the compilation since its contents weren't part of any particular play but were instead little bits that I'd referred to as "mini-closet dramas," or, scenes meant to be read on the page rather than viewed on the stage; yet week after week, the sketches brought Klapper Hall's Cave of Spleen to a roar and Richard kept remarking on how he could easily see them turned into a stage production called *Selfies*. (It turns out, there was already a TV show on by that name but I was flattered just the same.) Although I'm still not sure how the installments in this collection (now known as *Cockloft*) would work in live theater, the class's enthusiasm for the project helped me to keep it going long after the semester had ended, primarily on my Facebook page, where it has developed somewhat of a cult following.

In her landmark book on creative writing, *Writing Down the Bones*, Natalie Goldberg gives some sage advice that I have taken to heart ever since I first stumbled upon it two decades ago:

> Give yourself some space before you decide to write those big volumes. Learn to trust the force of your own voice. Naturally, it will evolve a direction and a need for one, but it will come from a different place than your need to be an achiever. Writing is not a McDonald's hamburger. The cooking is slow, and in the beginning, you are not sure whether a roast or a banquet or a lamb chop will be the result. (Goldberg 48)

Under Goldberg's influence, I have indeed given myself *tremendous* space for writing over the years.

In my application letter for this program, as a matter of fact, I mentioned that, after both of my parents died, my brother UPS'd me the five or so years' worth of free-written notebooks that I'd stored in their crawlspace prior to my move to New York City. I also mentioned that, all together, the boxes of notebooks weighed over 150 pounds. In my 15 years in New York, I have probably filled up five times as many notebooks, all with the faith that this sort of "writing practice," as Goldberg calls it, is not only the best way for me to improve as a writer but also the best way for me to evolve the pieces that I'm meant to write.

However, it had been my assumption that after spending so many years in the notebooks, I would end up writing "those big volumes" that Goldberg refers to.

I'm talking, *War & Peace*, at least! Now, before I came to QC, I'd published and won awards for a 232-page novel called *85A* but any novel that I wrote after that *roman à clef* felt forced and did not make the grade, so back to the notebooks I went. And although I was writing all sorts of vignettes and dialogues *just for fun* on the side, I found that no more novels were issuing from all my notebook work. I felt as though my writing life was becoming nothing more than a colossal waste of time.

So off to grad school I went, thinking the experience would steer me back on to the novel-writing course. And I did indeed write a novella called *Cash and the Chicken Hero* as my final project for Jeffrey Cassvan's Literary Theory course in my first year. Yet it wasn't until I took Nicole Cooley's Tiny Texts class, in the second semester of the second year of the program, that it dawned on me that, after decades of hardcore practice, my writing wasn't seeking to take the form of epic novels or full-length plays or even standard-sized short stories. Instead, my writing had long been taking the form of what Nicole calls "tiny texts"—flash pieces, short personal essays and quick exchanges.

At first, I did not take this to be good news. Here I felt as though I'd pushed myself past the point of exhaustion getting all the necessary ingredients together to cook the most sumptuous banquet I could prepare, only to put everything into the magic oven of creativity and find that, when I opened the oven door, all that was coming out were mini-pizza bagels! And, yes, pizza is my favorite food but are mini-pizza bagels *substantial* enough? After long and agonizing bouts of soul-searching, I have found myself going over to the Leonard Cohen camp and saying, "*Eff* 'substantial enough'! Write what *wants* to be written. Write what grows naturally from your own inmost soul."

Most of my dialogues with Julius and other personages in *Cockloft* were transcribed only moments after they occurred. We'd be chatting away about one thing or another and I'd get a *spanda*, an intuitive hit, that would tell me, "Write that one down." From there, I'd pull out my phone, type up the exchange and either post it on social media or save it in my email drafts. Often I've gone back to such pieces years later and been surprised to find that I wouldn't change them all that much; I'd been able to capture the original spirit as soon as it'd hit. Bob Dylan expressed a similar sentiment about his own songwriting in a 1991 interview with Paul Zollo:

> The best songs to me—my best songs—are songs which were written very quickly. Yeah, very, very quickly. Just about as much time as it takes to write it down is about as long as it takes to write it. (Hedin 213)

As we all know, Bob Dylan won the Nobel Prize for Literature in 2016. If he can see the value in this catch-it-by-the-tail kind of writing, then maybe I've been on to something with how I've pounced on the pieces that have come to me in the writing of *Cockloft*.

In the summer of 2017, Jill Dearman, LAMBDA-award-winning author of the novel *The Great Bravura*, edited the initial manuscript for *Cockloft*, which she encouraged me to market as "*Seinfeld* meets Sedaris for iPhone readers." If we want to get even snazzier, we could call it, "*Seinfeld* meets Sedaris in the Snapchat Age," as one *Cockloft* piece quickly disappears into the next as if it were part of a thread of Snapchat messages.

In her notes, Jill also said the manuscript was especially timely because, although gay marriage itself had already become a "big ole nothing special on the menu" by the end of the Obama era, we are now living in a time where a de facto despot and his theocratic sidekick have LGBT rights in their crosshairs. There's a discernible panic that ensues in the collection as it moves from life under President Obama into life under the Trump administration, a regime that continuously threatens our civil liberties and indeed life on this planet. As the pieces in this thesis show, I was in London during the Brexit vote and I was in New York on the night of Hillary Clinton's tragic defeat. I saw the beginning of the end from dawn to dusk.

Yet for all this, *Cockloft* remains a comedy, a way to pick ourselves back up and keep going even as we are being politically undermined. D.H. Lawrence perfectly describes this sort of defiant resolve in the opening paragraph to *Lady Chatterley's Lover*:

> Ours is essentially a tragic age, so we refuse to take it tragically. The cataclysm has happened, we are

> among the ruins, we start to build up new little habitats, to have new little hopes. It is rather hard work: there is no smooth road into the future: but we go round, or scramble over the obstacles. We've got to live, no matter how many skies have fallen. (Lawrence 1)

Something the Swiss video artist Pipilotti Rist said in an interview has helped to give me some perspective on how to keep joy alive during a dark period in history such as our own. "Here in Europe," Rist said, "It's not hip to cultivate joy because pain counts *a priori* as more profound. I'm a great fan of evoking joy, ease, lightness. Because the opposite comes about by itself (Kennedy 2)." For better or for worse, as a full-blooded Irish-American author who has attended far too many wakes in my time, I recognize that humor is the antidote to despair so I'm instinctively inclined to pull my narratives back from the edge of the cliff.

The nonsense literature of Woody Allen, Patrick Dennis and Lewis Carroll has been a vital inspiration for me in this regard. "Mudder" is but one example of the many New York-y, Woody Allen sorts of exchanges that crackle throughout this thesis:

MUDDER

(*Kyle walks past a contractor on 8th Av, Brooklyn.*)

CONTRACTOR: (*on cell phone*) So, he starts givin' me this cock-n'-balls story -

KYLE: (*interloping*) That's cock-and-bull story.

CONTRACTOR: D'ya mind? I'm tawkin' to my mudder.

As for Patrick Dennis, author of *Auntie Mame*, I have long admired how he is able to combine high culture and deep camp at every level of Mame's multidimensional character and that of her Manhattan milieu. Although neither Julius nor I have ever sought to pattern our lives after the characters in Dennis's ingenious novel, it just so happens that I can't help but be the wisecracking, offbeat ham that I am as Julius dexterously negotiates his own double life as a hard-nosed businessman and bon vivant whose tastes are better suited to Honoré de Balzac's time than Justin Bieber's, and yet here we both find ourselves together, which is why one of the opening epigraphs to *Cockloft* is something that the character Stella (Thelma Ritter) says to Jimmy Stewart in a movie that dates back to the same epoch as *Auntie Mame*, Alfred Hitchcock's *Rear Window*: "When I married Miles, we were both a couple of maladjusted misfits. We are still maladjusted misfits, and we have loved every minute of it (Yanal 157)."

Cockloft also shares some DNA with *Alice's Adventures in Wonderland* and *Through the Looking-*

Glass in that these are texts in which the protagonist wanders from one scenario to the next, trying to make heads or tails of her own and everyone else's idiosyncrasies, something you'll often find myself and others doing throughout my thesis, as in these lines from "An Attractive Nuisance":

JULIUS: She had a nice handbag and clean clothes. She even put some tissue under her so she wouldn't wet her pants.

KYLE: How does putting tissues under yourself keep you from wetting your pants?

JULIUS: You know what I mean. Getting her pants wet.

KYLE: Well, why didn't you say that then?—So what'd you say to her?

JULIUS: I said, "What are you doing?" She said, "I'm rolling a cigarette." I said, "But you don't live here." She said, "We all live somewhere."

KYLE: Did you tell her that's a straw-man argument?

JULIUS: I did. But she said, "What's a straw-man argument?" So, I started giving her examples but she kept acting like she didn't know what I was talking about.

KYLE: Yeah, people who make straw-man arguments do that a lot.

While we're on the subject of Lewis Carroll, it occurs to me that the writing in *Cockloft* finds a subtle validation, if not inspiration, from a certain literary technique that Annemarie Drury lectures on in her Victorian Poetry class, where I wrote a 36-page paper on Darwinian tropes in the poems in *Alice in Wonderland*. One such technique is "narrative suspension," which Alfred Lord Tennyson employs to great effect. In his poems "Mariana," "The Lady of Shalott," and "The Lotos-Eaters," for example, Tennyson sets the stage by taking classic scenes from canonical texts, building elaborate settings, introducing his readers to classic characters—and then bringing the narrative momentum to a halt by making the subjects' emotional lives the center of his poems. Mariana from *Measure for Measure* takes to her bed and bemoans the absence of her lover; The Lady of Shalott drifts down the river to Camelot and dies because the world outside her chambers is too much for her; Ulysses' troops eat the Lotos plant, an opiate, and drift off into oblivion rather than returning to the high seas. Although I am not a poet and I do not tend to build elaborate settings or draw from classic scenes or characters in *Cockloft*, the narratives do employ a certain "narrative suspension" in as much as they serve up only a sliver or a slice rather than the whole saga of my own life or of my life with Julius. Taken together, these quick sketches add up to portraiture.

Now, I'm often asked, "Are these dialogues true? Did they really happen?" To which I reply, "They're, erm… lightly edited for clarity," or, as Ken Kesey famously remarked about the events in *One Flew Over the Cuckoo's Nest*: "It's true even if it didn't happen (Leeds 134)." *Or*, there's what the character Jackie O'Shea tells his Irish village in the 1998 movie, *Waking Ned Devine*: "I mean,

I've been known to add a little color to stories and riddles for the benefit of those who will listen." The way I see it: not only am I Irish, but I'm also a fiction writer, both of which give me license to waver from fact—at least for the purposes of this thesis.

Yet there is another dimension to my writing process, beyond compulsive notebook writing and spontaneous smartphone compositions, and that is the process of meditation. I have been practicing meditation, mostly in Theravada and Mahayana traditions of Buddhism, for the past 20 years and have found it to be an invaluable support in taking stock of my own life experience and in generating new narratives. Meditation enables us to slow down and open our consciousness to the spontaneous arising of all manner of thoughts, emotions, memories, sensations and impressions—from our basest urges to our hearts' most profound wisdom. Not only can this compost of images and ideas that accrues over the course of a steady practice of meditation become the raw material for our own creative ventures but it is also through meditation that we train in becoming more mindful toward the events of our own daily lives, which are themselves fertile loam for writing. Although the expressionist painter Paul Klee did not engage in a formal process of meditation, according to his friend Lyonel Feininger, he did cultivate a good deal of mindful awareness as part of his creative process:

> His method of working can really be compared to the organic development of a plant. There was something akin to magic in the process. For hours, he

> would sit quietly in a corner smoking, apparently not occupied at all but full of inner watching. Then he would rise and quietly, with unerring sureness, he would add a touch of color here, draw a line or spread a tone there thus attaining his vision with infallible logic, in an almost unconscious way. (Gayford 31)

In much the same way, meditation has aided me in attuning to and enlarging upon the moments that have made *Cockloft* possible.

Also consonant with the dharma (the teachings of the Buddha) and meditation practice is the matter of impermanence, a central motif in the emerging "flash" genre of literature, which many of *Cockloft*'s pieces fit squarely into. The Buddha told his students that the most important thing for them to understand, above and beyond even the *brahmavihra* of compassion or the Eightfold Path, is the concept of *annica*, or, impermanence:

> Better a single day of life perceiving how things rise and fall than to live out a century yet not perceiving their rise and fall. (Dhammapada 113)

Now, why would impermanence be the most important thing for us to understand? A big reason is that we too often go about our lives thinking we have forever. Impermanence reminds us that all things are in a constant state of flux, that there is *nothing* we can hold on to for long—not our victories, not our fortunes, not our own lives, not the lives of those we cherish most. This is why I have chosen to begin my brisk-clipped, mostly "flash" thesis with this quote from the Tibetan master, H.E. Chagdud Tulku Rinpoche:

> Our relationships with one another are like a chance meeting of two strangers in a parking lot. They look at each other and smile. That is all there is between them. They leave and never see each other again. That is what life is—just a moment, a passing and then it is gone. (Chagdud Tulku 91)

We could either be depressed about the reality of impermanence or we could celebrate that we have been privileged to have these brief moments of connection with other beings, just as the character Emily does when she emerges as a ghost, peering in on her family, at the end of Thornton Wilder's *Our Town*:

> Oh, Mama, just look at me for one minute as if you really saw me. Mama, fourteen years have gone by. I'm dead. You're a grandmother, Mama... Wally's dead too. Mama, his appendix burst on a camping trip to North Conway. We felt just terrible about

it—don't you remember? But just for a moment we're all together. Mama, just for a moment we're happy. *Let's look at one another . . .* I didn't realize. All that was going on in life and we never noticed…Oh, earth, you're too wonderful for anyone to realize you. *(She asks abruptly through her tears)* Do any human beings ever realize life while they live it? (Wilder 97-100)

Cockloft seeks to celebrate the fleeting moments of connection that I, the author, have been so fortunate to have had with Julius and so many other beings—friends, family, animals and strangers alike.

Throughout the time that I have been posting installments from *Cockloft* on Facebook, I have also been avidly following Brandon Stanton's photoblog *Humans of New York*, which is nothing less than a bastion for humanity in a world of increasing impersonality. In this series, Stanton stops random people in the street, takes their pictures and asks them to tell him something about their lives. Millions of viewers, including former President Barack Obama, who is a huge fan of Stanton's work and has himself been featured on the site, scroll through to see a passerby stop to share only a whisper of their experience, a whisper that might cause us to erupt in laughter or dissolve into tears. Such is the power of the anecdote, and *Humans of New York* has reaffirmed for me that there is value in producing what is essentially a collection of anecdotes for my final project.

In this anecdotal spirit, I'd like to conclude by paraphrasing an old chestnut from Ricky Gervais, British comedian and co-creator of the BBC series, *The Office*, which was of course adapted to great success in a sitcom by the same name in the United States. A *Fast Company* interviewer asked Gervais what has been the greatest influence on his creative-writing process. With his usual cheek, Gervais demurred to give a response but then settled down and wistfully shared that his greatest influence to date has been the English teacher he had when he was 14 years old.

When the teacher would give the class a creative-writing assignment, Gervais would get all excited and write up thrillers that featured lots of explosions and high body counts just like the police procedurals he'd see on TV. He was sure he'd get good grades for them but when the teacher would hand his stories back to him, they'd be covered in red marks, cross-outs and the mandate, "Write what you know." Gervais decided that, if this was how the teacher wanted it, he'd go ahead and write him the most boring story he could think of.

So, one day, Gervais decided to tag along with his mother who would go down the road several times a week to help an old lady out with some housework. What could be more boring than that? Gervais thought, and so he took notes as he watched his mother go about her chores in the old woman's home. "The house smells like tea and lavender and mold," he wrote. He also noted the menial tasks that his mother performed, jotted down the unremarkable lines from the unremarkable exchanges he'd witnessed her having with the old woman and wove his notes into a throwaway narrative that he turned in as homework.

Later that week, his teacher walked in between the rows of desks, handing everybody back their stories. Except he did not hand Gervais back his story. He *whipped* it back at him. Gervais groaned and flipped the paper over to see what kind of an abysmal grade he got this time. There at the top of the page stood a big red "A." Young Ricky Gervais' head jerked up and his teacher gave him a nod. Gervais says, "It was the proudest moment of my life…Trying to make the ordinary extraordinary is so much better than starting with the extraordinary."

Gervais' plan to bore his teacher to death might have backfired but it was by no means a misfire. Neither was his mockumentary series on the dreary lives of office workers, which he'd grow up to co-create with Stephen Merchant. On the contrary, it became a BBC classic, as well as an international franchise.

With this in mind, welcome to my own quotidian labor of love.

Step into my *Cockloft*.

It may not be a masterpiece but I do have some mini-pizza bagels fresh out of the oven in case you're hungry.

June 2018
San Francisco, CA

WORKS CITED

Chagdud Tulku Rinpoche. *Life in Relation to Death.* Chennai, India: Padma Publishing House, 2000. Second Edition

Dhamapada, verse 113: http://www.tipitaka.net/tipitaka/dhp/verseload.php?verse=113

Gayford, Martin. *Feat of Klee, Bonhams* Magazine, Issue 44, Autumn 2015.

Gervais, Ricky. *Fast Company*: "Ricky Gervais Tells a Story About How He Learned to Write," https://www.youtube.com/watch?v=zTJyDe7a2bo

Goldberg, Natalie. *Writing Down the Bones: Freeing the Writer Within.* Boulder: Shambhala Publishing. 1988, 2014, 2016. Kindle Edition.

Hedin, Benjamin. *Studio A: The Bob Dylan Reader.* New York, London: W.W. Norton & Company, 2005.

Kennedy, Randy. "Pipilotti Rist, Provoking with Delight," *The New York Times*, October 21, 2016

Lawrence, D.H. *Lady Chatterley's Lover.* Blacksburg, VA: Wilder Publications, Inc.

2010. Kindle Editions

Leeds, Barry H. *Modern Literature Series: Ken Kesey*. New York: Frederick Ungar

Publishing Company. First Edition, 1981.

Leibovitz, Liel. *A Broken Hallelujah: Rock and Roll, Redemption and the Life of Leonard*

Cohen. New York, London: W.W. Norton & Company, 2014.

Waking Ned Devine, quotes: http://www.imdb.com/title/tt0166396/quotes

Wilder, Thornton. *Our Town*. New York: Harper Publishing, 1938, 1957.

Yanal, Robert. *Hitchcock as Philosopher. Jefferson, North Carolina: McFarland*

Publishing, 2005.

Kyle Thomas Smith is the author of the multi-award-winning novel 85A. He lives in Brooklyn and San Francisco with his husband Julius and their cats, Giuseppe and Giacomo. You can contact him, the only man still on Yahoo Mail, at shugakyle@yahoo.com (an awful email address from the 1990s that won't go away and that he'll never live down).

ACKNOWLEDGMENTS

Thank you, Nicole Cooley, Richard Schotter, Roger Sedarat and Jill Dearman, for your encouragement and editorial direction. Thank you, Caitlin Meyer, for equating my silly posts with art when I was in the throes of *The Shining*-level writer's block. Thank you to my dear friends Victor Melenhorst, Amah-Rose Abrams McKnight and Jane "Ellan Vannin" Davis for being such stellar overseas advisors for this project. To my best man, Mike Levine—what can I say, so many pieces in this book were born from our texting and, if it weren't for you, THC would be just three random all-cap letters to me. Thank you, Martin Aylward, for your wit and spiritual direction and for showing me that pizzazz need not be the far enemy of Theravada Buddhism. Thank you, Jose Antonio Sanchez Kinghorn and Jacqui Henao, for your friendship and support of this project and for filming the inaugural *Cockloft* reading. Thank you, Felix Matos Rodriguez, for your friendship and guidance throughout grad school. Thank you, Maria Fischinger and Joey and Alexandra Fish, for letting me know that *Cockloft* is a title even straight people can love. Thank you, Nick Campanella, for your wonderful, typewritten critique that convinced me to make this my thesis. Thank you, Tosha B. Silver, for your constant counsel and for reminding me to offer up all this material (and everything else too). Thank you, Karim El Dada, for the goldmine of material that our bull sessions and your colleagues provided for me in the writing of this book. Thank you to our dear departed and dearly beloved cat Marquez for letting me know that it's not only okay but perfectly natural to like cats better than people—and to our fantabulous felines Giuseppe and Giacomo for making this tangled yarn ball we call existence so much more hilarious than it already is. Thank you to Drs. St-Vincent, Jacovino, Camps, Palma and Vincent at Animal Medical Center and Animal Kind for the near-miraculous work you did on our guys in situations that were truly life or death. Thank you, Adam Paul Jones and Clara Longobardo, for our time in Livorno and for getting me to finally write "Palle." Thank you, Brad M. Gray and Enrico Icchi Giolo (I'd plum forgotten about SophiaLoRent until that night at Seraghina). Thank you, Dinesh Rajawasan, for your hospitality in Sri Lanka. Thank you, Nicola Fabens, for opening the window to a squirrel-free future for our home. Thank you, Pascal St-Pierre, for your friendship and loyalty through the years and throughout the writing of this book. Thank you, Armen Meyer, for letting me know I was on to something with all this minutiae. Thank you, Jennifer Harris, for your friendship and encouragement through the years and the early drafts of the essays in this book.

Finally, I'd like to thank Julius without whom the pages of this book, and indeed the whole of life, would be empty, meaningless and blank—there are no words or limits for my love.

Made in the USA
Monee, IL
12 February 2026

44089479R00177